D1435697

Copyright® 2020 by Scott Harris
All rights reserved. No part of this publication
may be reproduced or transmitted in any form or
by any means, electronic or mechanical, including
photocopying, recording, scanning or otherwise,
or through any information browsing, storage or
retrieval system, without permission in writing
from the publisher.

**MY WOW**

This book is dedicated to George Spears, a man that inspired me, challenged me, and loved me from the age of 10 until today. I miss you George.

**Donall George Spears
(1950 - 2015)**

# CREATE WOW
## CUSTOMER EXPERIENCES: CX 2.0

BY SCOTT HARRIS

## TABLE OF CONTENTS

| | Introduction | 9 |
|---|---|---|
| Ch. 1 | A Box to Check | 12 |
| Ch. 2 | Your Brand | 19 |
| Ch. 3 | Your Culture | 25 |
| Ch. 4 | Experience Evolution | 33 |
| Ch. 5 | NPS: Not Particularly Sufficient | 43 |
| Ch. 6 | The CX 2.0 Shift | 54 |
| Ch. 7 | Rule #1: Focus on the Most Impactful Interactions | 67 |
| Ch. 8 | Rule #2: Start with Behavior | 75 |
| Ch. 9 | Rule #3: Know and Drive Business Outcomes | 89 |
| Ch. 10 | Rule #4: Wherever Possible, Automate | 99 |
| Ch. 11 | Rule #5: Escalate and Resolve Issues | 110 |
| Ch. 12 | Rule #6: Manage Content and Consistent Data | 124 |
| Ch. 13 | Rule #7: Collect and Share Feedback | 138 |
| Ch. 14 | Rule #8: Create a Virtuous Cycle | 148 |
| Ch. 15 | Rule #9: Make Data-Driven Decisions | 154 |
| Ch. 16 | A Top-Tier U.S. Rental Car Company | 160 |
| Ch. 17 | New American Funding | 178 |
| Ch. 18 | Designing Your CX 2.0 Strategy | 188 |
| Ch. 19 | Your Hometown Pharmacy | 199 |
| Ch. 20 | The Next Salesforce | 208 |
| | Appendix | 217 |
| | Author Biography | 223 |
| | Acknowledgments | 225 |
| | Index | 229 |

## INTRODUCTION
# Create WOW Customer Experiences

Experience management ideas and technologies have evolved and will continue to do so. This book explores that evolution and lands on a set of ideas that define its future. The more you understand the management, data collection and analysis of Customer Experience (CX), Employee Experience (EX), and enterprise reputation, the more "Aha!" moments you will have as you read.

Before we begin, it's also important to note there are many customer experience interaction types. We will briefly discuss these and their importance within your strategy. We will, however, focus mostly on human interactions. CX

2.0 is not a new standardized mathematical scoring model. It is a method of driving behavior, improving experiences, powering culture and brand, all while collecting far more CX data than any other method. CX 2.0 simply means Customer Experience, evolved. Therefore, your current state is your new benchmark. Thinking about your performance in comparison to others should be more of a celebration of your dominance than an inspection of your likeness to your competitors. They won't be able to keep up.

During the past five years, we have been lucky enough to start in the right business verticals, build great technology, and gather a tribe of hundreds of fantastic marketers and executives. Thanks to the many who contributed to the stories and ideas found herein.

Welcome to the tribe. Enjoy!

## CX Tribe

At the end of each chapter you will find a section titled CX Tribe. It outlines the focus and potential challenges of the chapter and what to expect as you continue.

Take it personally. A few chapters are for information only. Others are meant to challenge you and create opportunities to improve. In a conversation with one of the editors, I asked him how the "Your Brand" chapter felt. He said, "It didn't feel good." I asked why and he responded, "I have a lot of work to do at my company." He took it personally. You do the same.

Let's begin...

CHAPTER ONE

# A Box to Check

C raig, an executive at ACME Enterprises, gets a call from Fred, his top sales guy. Fred says, "I lost a big deal, because of our Google reviews." Ouch! Craig is not happy. He runs down the hall and quickly sticks his head into the office of Stephanie, the head of marketing. "Steph, what's up with all these Google reviews? We just missed out on a massive deal that we couldn't afford to lose. Fix it!"

And there it is—a box to check.

## ACME Enterprises ✕

| Website | Directions | Save |

2.3 ★★★ ★ ★ 272 Google reviews
General Business Oakland, California

**Address:** 123 Main Street, Anywhere USA, 98765
**Hours: Open** · Closes 11:59PM ▾
Labor Day might affect these hours
**Phone:** (555) 254-4410

Suggest an edit · Manage this listing 🌐

The biggest mistake companies make is solving problems one at a time—literally checking one box after the other. This is how the reputation management world started. Companies work on one problem at a time, check one box and then move on to the next. But checking a box is not the same thing as finding a solution. In this example, Craig wants to "fix" the company's Google reviews. He has no visibility past the problem in front of him. He wants happy customers writing Google reviews.

"Fix it!" That's usually how it starts. That's also the reason many marketers choose solutions that limit their outcomes. Stephanie needs to fix the company's Google reviews, so she hires a software partner that focuses on creating Google reviews to check this box.

Six months later, ACME opens up its 15th retail storefront. Stephanie notices the business listings for many of the locations have inaccurate or inconsistent data. For example, her Danville, CA location shows 723 Becker Street on Yelp. That's an old address. Bing and Yahoo have the correct address information, but both use an old 1-800 number. In fact, there are more than 100 online listings for the Danville location and none of them perfectly match the ACME website. Stephanie has another box to check. This time, she goes with a SaaS partner who has a premium business listings distribution product.

A few months later, Craig is in a board meeting and the board wants deeper insights from the customer base. Brian, the chair of the board, has a lot of experience with NPS[1] reports and wants to see how ACME stacks up against the competition. For this, they choose a data analytics partner known for business intelligence reporting. Brian has worked with them in the past, so it was an easy choice. Another box checked.

After a few months with customer survey insights, Craig, Brian and the board realize they have an employee engagement problem. This time they need an employee survey to collect employee sentiment and will likely need an employee engagement partner. Good news, their data

[1] Net Promoter, Net Promoter System, Net Promoter Score, NPS and the NPS-related emoticons are registered trademarks of Bain & Company, Inc., Fred Reichheld and Satmetrix Systems, Inc.

analytics partner has an employee survey. It's an additional fee, but they won't need another vendor. Next they hire an employee engagement consultancy to help motivate their workforce to perform at their best and deploy a pay-for-performance culture. Yet another box is checked.

I could go on and on about all the boxes that get checked one by one. We haven't discussed employee scorecards, brand mentions, social monitoring, third-party review sites beyond Google, or omni-channel data and AI. Check, check, check, check . . . and functions that should work together become siloed. ACME selects software, hires people to manage it, spends money, reacts to the problem of the day and checks box after box, one at a time.

IT'S ALL WRONG!

ALL OF THESE PROBLEMS ARE THE SAME PROBLEM!

They are a part of a single puzzle. Piece it together and you will discover a beautiful picture of your company—happy employees and happy customers partnering as advocates and fanatics for your brand. It is a picture of consistent data for all locations and lots of happy customer reviews everywhere. Each of the individual providers are checking a box. Put them together and you have an experience strategy. Evolving your ideas and seeing it as a single problem will create better outcomes than any of the box checking solutions could individually.

Experience Management is not a list of individual problems and solutions. It is a single puzzle. When it is put together properly, each piece works far more efficiently than it possibly could as an individual solution.

Craig wanted to fix his Google reviews so he would stop losing business. What he didn't know was that he should be focused on putting together a complete, interconnected strategy. Instead, the ACME Enterprises team took two years and spent millions of dollars checking boxes, only to build siloed technologies and teams.

Which pieces of the puzzle are you addressing with siloed technologies? Which are a part of integrated systems? If you are just beginning to build a strategy, then you are in luck. Building a strategy from scratch can be far easier than trying to off-board technology and start over. Software companies know that even mediocre technology can be sticky, especially for bigger companies. That is why many software companies focus on building scale more than improving product.

Siloed technologies are often managed by different stakeholders within the organization. The head of HR may start kicking and screaming if you try to remove software they have been using for years. Department heads and their teams often protect their domains and stay with bad tech because of a relationship with the vendor, familiarity with the product, or any number of other reasons. You may find yourself building a highly integrated strategy and only deploying a few pieces of the puzzle at a time. Winning over the long haul may not be perfect, but it is still winning.

## CX Tribe

It is one problem. It is all connected: culture, brand, reputation, retention, recruiting, loyalty, engagement, and behavior. They are all leaves on the same, very leafy tree.

Make a list of all of your experience box-checking solutions. Add to this list any solutions that employees or locations are using individually. How are you collecting employee feedback? Customer feedback? How are you managing location data accuracy? What about online or third-party sites like Google My Business? How are you managing your professional and business listings websites? Are you monitoring the internet for company or executive mentions? Are you analyzing calls, chat, Q&A and tickets for insights?

Later, we will define the rules and methods for designing and implementing your strategy. But first, let's do a quick exercise I call the "personification of brand." How healthy is your brand? Let's find out.

CHAPTER TWO
# Your Brand

Imagine your company as a living entity—it can breathe, walk, run, eat, smile, laugh, cry, and even make friends. Now, imagine it in front of a mirror, staring at its reflection. What does it see?

Is it male or female? Is it a child, teenager, young adult, middle-aged, or closing in on retirement? Is it vibrant and full of energy, or lethargic and barely scooting along? Is it happy, sanguine, bitter, sad? Is it skinny, fit, a little plump or downright overweight? Is it confident and secure, or not so much? What else do you know about this business reflection?

Is it a world traveler, or does it stay close to home? Is it a planner, or a little reactive? Does it bring people together, or pull them apart? Does it make you feel safe? Is it fun to be around, or are people counting the hours until they get away? Does it attract great people? Does it have many friends?

The company's friends include its employees, customers, investors, and vendors. How would they describe this living entity that is your company? Do the employees see empowerment, excitement and purpose? Or do they only see a means to an end? Do vendors love the partnership and feel like a part of the team? Or do they feel like a supplier, never appreciated or acknowledged for their part in its success? Are the investors proud of what they've helped build, or are they worried about recouping their investment? Do customers see a company that they can count on and want to promote, or one that doesn't deliver on its promises?

As an example, let's answer these questions about my company. It is young and vibrant. It is not yet as fit as it can be. It is mostly confident, but insecurities do come up from time to time. It travels the U.S. and soon the world. It is both a planner and a little reactive—at times a lot reactive. It brings people together, but doesn't yet make them feel completely safe. It is fun to be around. It attracts great people and has a lot of friends.

As for those friends…

Employees at our company feel like they are a part of something big and exciting. Coming to work is never a chore. Vendors feel like partners and are appreciated for their part in its success. Investors are excited, but cautious. And customers feel like they are a part of the business. We are a tribe.

Take a minute and write this description for your company. Be as honest with yourself as possible. Maybe you should ask employees to do the exercise as well. What do you see? What does this say about your company, your future, and your brand? This is an exercise that should be completed periodically as it is in constant flux. A single employee or customer can have a big impact on the results.

Let's take a minute to define what "brand" means. Zappos founder Tony Hsieh wrote in his book *Delivering Happiness: A Path to Profits, Passion, and Purpose* that "a company's culture and a company's brand are two sides of the same coin. The brand is simply a lagging indicator of the culture." Marty Neumeier, author and speaker on all things brand, defines it like this: "A brand is not a logo. A brand is not an identity. A brand is not a product. A brand is a person's gut feeling about a product, service or organization." In other words, a brand is whatever customers and employees believe and feel it is.

Now, with this in mind, let's look at a well known company— Subway—through this lens. If I asked a Subway executive to describe their brand, how would they respond? Likely they would say that their brand is "Eat Fresh." They might tell you about their animal welfare policy or their commitment to community. They would definitely want you to know about the entrepreneurial independence of their franchise owners.

But is "Eat Fresh" really their brand? Or is their brand actually the answers to the "personification of brand" exercise above? What do you believe and feel when you hear Subway? This means that the brand is no longer what the company says it is. It is what the customers, employees, vendors, and partners believe and feel it is.

In my career, I have interviewed hundreds of potential employees. I often ask brand questions about their previous employment experiences. The majority of these prospective employees tell me that their previous companies have a set of values, but never really live them. "Yes, we have core values, but the company looks nothing like that to any of our employees or customers." When I ask if they can recite any of their core values or mission statement from memory, I often get a blank stare. One guy said, "Have fun … I think. Although the place was not much fun."

A company's brand is a living thing. It is constantly in flux. It is either getting better or worse, rarely staying consistent.

## CX Tribe

We are executives, marketers and leaders. We spend significant time and resources designing, developing, and promoting the brand we hope will resonate with our customers. How are you doing? Is the brand you are promoting aligned with what your customers and employees think it is?

Complete the "personification of brand" exercise. Get three or more members of your leadership team to do the exercise. Go over it in a leadership meeting or do it with an anonymous form. Compare the answers. Ask a few location managers to do the exercise. Compare the answers. Ask several employees for their opinions. What did you learn? Was your description the same as others?

What about the other side of Tony Hsieh's coin, culture? Let's explore...

CHAPTER THREE

# Your Culture

The ROI for a brand with a great reputation can be 100 times or more. It impacts market value and is a powerful driver of shareholder returns. Reputation can create new business, validate referrals, help you recruit and retain great employees, and also improve search rankings, customer satisfaction and brand perception.

Your reputation is both internal and external. It starts with your core ideas and ends with how you execute on those ideas for your employees and customers. Two companies selling the exact same products will inspire vastly different loyalties from their customers and employees based on this execution.

This week, I counted the number of shoes in my house. We have more than 150 pairs. I estimate that our household purchases over 50 pairs a year. When there are five children, a grandchild, and a son-in-law all living under your roof, you have a lot of shoes. The kids are into soccer, tennis, golf, and Tae Kwon Do. More shoes. Where do we buy our shoes? Marshalls, Nordstrom Rack, Amazon, and Target. It's a commodity business. You buy them anywhere and everywhere. There are literally thousands of retail shoe stores and hundreds more online. But there is only one Zappos. Zappos sells the same Nike's I purchased at Macy's. They have those same slip-on checkered Vans that my kids love.

Vans Classic Slip-On™ Core Classics

★★★★★ 3,551 Reviews

How then did Zappos, a seller of shoes, build a $900 million online shoe store? Culture! It is an extremely complicated mission. They made a decision to "Deliver WOW" experiences for customers and employees. And they live it, through the good and the bad.

When Zappos outsourced shipping, they had outsourced a core piece of the "Deliver WOW" promise, so it didn't work. They fixed it. Their leadership models WOW. They train WOW. They execute on WOW. As Tony says, "Two sides of the same coin." They have created a billion-dollar shoe store by WOWing customers, employees, and partners. These customers return to the scene of the WOW. That is why 75% of Zappos business is repeat customers, month over month. That kind of loyalty is valuable—Amazon thought it was worth 10 million shares, equal to $880 million, when they purchased Zappos in 2009.

"WOW" is a small word, but it sets a big expectation. It means that they go above and beyond for their customers, co-workers, partners, vendors, and investors. Zappos takes their focus on WOW to the next level by publishing the annual Zappos Culture Book. Every employee gets to describe the company's culture in their own words, and it is published as written.

Zappos focuses internally on the WOW. It is how they recruit, train, and retain great staff and ultimately define the company's brand. They built a billion-dollar mail order shoe store by focusing on their WOW.

**DELIVER WOW THROUGH SERVICE**
CORE VALUE #1

Too often, instead of focusing on culture, we are forced to look at culture and brand through a reputation filter. It starts with an external headache—like bad reviews on Google or Yelp hurting the business. Of course, companies want happy customers writing reviews to cancel out the few unhappy customers' reviews. And while you should react to this problem for short term gains, you also may need to address issues that may be at the root of the problem— what are your promises to your employees and customers? How are you executing on those promises?

No company is perfect. But a customer and employee strategy starts with culture. This is the core promise you make to your customers and employees. Think about the promise you make to your employees, your internal promise.

Do you know it? Do you live it? Do your employees know it? Are they experiencing it?

Here is an example of a possible internal promise and its potential impact on a company's culture:

> *"We will create a fun work experience with continuous opportunities for personal growth and career development."*

If this was your internal promise, how would you execute on it? What outcomes would it help create?

First, the bigger your company is, the more likely you would need a full-time resource focusing on it. This promise could include weekly happy hours, afternoon activities like volleyball games, and family-style movie nights. You would likely begin investing in personal development and promoting from within. You may even want to create your own culture book.

By executing on this promise, you would see a big lift on your internal and external reputation. Recruiting would benefit accordingly, and you would see a measurable improvement in retention rates. This would create a level of employee engagement which would lead directly to happier customers and improved products and services. Your internal promise would have some pretty fantastic external benefits.

As an example of an external promise, let's use my company's. We have two:

*"We are marketers building technology together" and "Create WOW"*

The first, "We are marketers building technology together" has led us to develop a Partner Advisory Board and an annual marketing and culture event, The Create WOW Summit. Nearly half of our customers come together each year to celebrate their successes and help us ideate the future of our platform. Our development process always starts and ends with our customers' voices.

Our "Create WOW" promise is our internal and external promise. Wowing our customers requires a one-to-one relationship, which occurs through our white glove Customer Success Team. It demands that we continue to add to the platform and deliver more value than promised. It comes with a continual improvement standard. We constantly check and challenge our features, adoption and execution and have developed a gap analysis exercise to make sure customers are getting every benefit possible.

Often we have a customer that is extremely happy and a big promoter of our company, but we are still unhappy with our execution. We usually want more for our customers than they themselves are ready to deploy.

These promises have a big impact on our business. They have led to a massive tribe-building exercise. Our team knows our customers by name. The executives often text me personally when they need something. Our external promise has internal benefits. Because of our internal and external promises, we are able to keep great employees, recruit new team members, and retain customers (tribe members).

## CX Tribe

What is your internal promise? How are you executing on that promise? Can you say with confidence that your internal promise drives your company culture and brand? Are your culture and brand two sides of the same coin? Execution can usually be measured by outcomes: How is your recruiting? Retention? Employee satisfaction? Employee-customer relationships?

Ask your team to do a 60-second video on your company's culture and what it means to them. Meet with leadership and watch the videos. How many employees were willing to do the exercise? How many opted out? (Opt-outs can be a bad signal). What did they say? Brainstorm a list of possible initiatives that could impact company culture and align with your internal promise. Which one of these things should you do first? Which would have the biggest impact? Which do you have the resources and time to do?

Before we begin designing campaigns together later in the book, let's go backwards and explore the evolution of the experience economy and the impact of popular (and very convenient) online shopping experiences.

CHAPTER FOUR

# Experience Evolution

F rom the great depression in the '30s and WWII in the '40s all the way until today, we have evolved into an experience-driven society. If it saves us time, keeps us active, entertains us, makes us feel good, inspires us, or whatever, we will pay for it. In order to have the best experiences, we have developed systems that we trust. Today we have reviews and referrals. In the near future, we will have advanced sentiment analysis data alongside videos of our friends sharing their insights popping up on our eyeglasses as we walk into or near a particular business.

## The Experience Economy

Harvard Business Review

INNOVATION

# Welcome to the Experience Economy

by B. Joseph Pine II and James H. Gilmore

FROM THE JULY-AUGUST 1998 ISSUE

In a 1998 issue of the *Harvard Business Review*, the innovative article "Welcome to the Experience Economy"[1] was published. The authors outlined the evolution of the Experience Economy and its impact on the progression of economic value. While they wrote this over 20 years ago, it is more relevant today than it was then.

In this insightful article, they used the evolution of the birthday cake as a model to explain the theory. Here is that story through my filter.

### Commodities

When my father was a child, his mother would take flour, butter, eggs, and sugar and make a cake. The finished product would likely have cost a couple of dimes.

---

[1] The Experience Economy: Work is Theater & Every Business a Stage - by B. Joseph Pine II & James H. Gilmore. http://bit.ly/CX20_Work; also Welcome to the Experience Economy by B. Joseph Pine II & James H. Gilmore. Harvard Business Review July-Aug 1998. http://bit.ly/cx2_experience

### Goods

When I was a child, my mother would buy Betty Crocker's boxed cake mix. She paid less than $1 for easy instructions, perfectly measured and mixed ingredients, and saved on time and mess.

### Services

When my first-born, Rebecca, was a toddler, I would go to the local grocery store bakery on her birthday and point to one of the cakes. Five minutes later, I could be walking out of the store with a personalized "Happy Birthday Becca" cake, featuring her favorite princess. Seemed like a bargain at $15.

### Experiences

Today, for my younger children, I will break the bank ($300+) for a birthday party experience, and they throw in the cake.

Imagine how today's reality would fit into any of the other eras. It wouldn't. In the '40s we were just emerging from the Great Depression and entering World War II. It is very hard to imagine bounce castle businesses and trampoline parks popping up on every corner in those days.

Even in the '70s, my mom made every family meal and baked every birthday cake. Going to dinner at Frisch's Big Boy in my hometown was a real treat and happened every second Friday. I am literally laughing out loud right now, thinking about my dad spending $300, or even $50, on a party in 1978 for me and my friends to jump on trampolines for an hour. Clearly, the evolution of economic value is a steep curve from then until now. Today, we value experiences and are happy to pay for them.

## The Amazon Effect

My 10-year-old son, Charlie, wanted DJ equipment for Christmas. So, he took to Amazon researching every kind of DJ equipment. He knows I am frugal so he sorted by price. Then, he found several options and dug into the reviews. When he came to me to make the ask, he was armed for victory. "Dad, I want a Pioneer DDJ-SB3 for Christmas. It's a DJ board. It's only $248 and I read the reviews," he said. "It has a 4.6 star rating with 187 reviews on Amazon and most

Pioneer DJ DJ Controller, Black (DDJ-SB3)
by Pioneer DJ
★★★★☆ ∨    187 customer reviews  |  290 answered questions
Amazon's Choice   for "pioneer ddj-sb3"

Price: $248.16 ✓prime FREE One-Day & FREE Returns

of the unhappy people just couldn't figure out how to use it." My 10-year-old knew exactly what he wanted, even though he had never used it or even seen it on a shelf. He is a different kind of buyer than me or my father. He relies on social proof. He loves that DJ board. He uses it constantly, most nights I wish our bedrooms didn't share a wall. I'm convinced that there are always dance parties going on in that room.

In many ways, his purchasing behavior is far better and more efficient than my own. Companies selling on Amazon are forced to listen to the voice of their customers and constantly improve their products and service levels. Customer experiences are in control of their success. Charlie doesn't like going to stores. He'd rather take 10 minutes and find the best product at the best price online. This is what I call the "Amazon Effect", and it further underlines the reality of the Experience Economy today and shows that customer experience drives business outcomes more today than ever before.

"Social Proof", a term coined by Robert Cialdini in his 1984 book *Influence,* is also known as informational social influence. It describes a psychological and social phenomenon wherein people copy the actions of others in an attempt to undertake behavior in a given situation.

## Local Business Impact

What about local retail stores, cafes, restaurants, or professional offices?

This year during spring break, I took the family to Newport Beach, CA. My 16 year-old daughter, Bailey, and my girlfriend, Emma, are both big coffee aficionados who love the coffee shop experience. While walking the boardwalk, Emma noticed a coffee shop and announced to Bailey that they should check it out. Without slowing her cadence on the walk, Bailey said, "Nah, I looked them up and they are only a 3.5."

Bailey spends a lot of (my) money on coffee. When we go anywhere, she searches for the best options. She never walked through the front door of the coffee shop, nor had she ever tasted their coffee, but they had already lost her business. Maybe her experience would have been fantastic. Maybe the shop just wasn't managing their online reputation. In any case, they likely lost $200, or more, of Bailey's and Emma's business over the course of the trip. Bailey needs social proof. She knows that coffee shops with a high volume (quantity) of great reviews (quality) and lots of product photos are likely to give her the best experience—and she values experiences.

***If you're not managing your online reputation, your unhappy customers are happy to do it for you.***

The people that went into that coffee shop had not taken the time to go online and say, "Eh…It's just ok." Just a minute down the boardwalk there was a better option. The better option got our business every day that week. The Newport Coffee Company was glad to take our eight morning orders: four hot chocolates, two lattes, one frappé-something or other, and my hot tea. In an Experience Economy, a company must not only provide awesome products and services, but they also must manage the online conversation. Imagine how impactful this could be for a local insurance company, lender, real estate company, or other professional? The coffee shop lost a few hundred dollars. How many millions in sales does a local real estate firm stand to lose?

Today, the customer is in charge and they want the best experiences. If they've never experienced working with your business, then they are likely to do a little research to find out if others enjoyed theirs.

## CX Tribe

How do your buyers find you? On a third-party site? Google? Yelp? A referral from a friend? An online directory? When they find you, what do they see?

Compose a fun internal survey and find out how your employees buy. It can give you some brilliant insights into the best ways to communicate and engage.

- *How are they entertained? Do they have cable, Netflix, Amazon Prime, YouTube, other?*
- *Do they read books or listen to them?*
- *Do they listen to music or prefer podcasts?*
- *Which do they prefer - a call, a text, an IM? Other?*
- *Do they get a newspaper, or read news online, or watch CNN or Fox?*
- *How did they find their last professional (loan officer, realtor, doctor, lawyer, dentist)?*
- *Do they get their groceries delivered or go*
- *to the store?*
- *How many online order (Amazon or other) boxes show up at their door per week?*
- *Do they belong to any mail or subscription services?*
- *Any other questions you can think of?*

We have one last step before we jump to the rules, designs, and stories of a great CX 2.0 strategy. No CX book would be complete without a good debate on NPS. How likely are you to refer...

CHAPTER FIVE

# NPS: Not Particularly Sufficient

How can you write a book on Customer Experience without discussing the ideas and systems that brought us here? Over the past three years, we have put the NPS question to the test and found it is no longer the only number you need to grow your business.

NPS is an old standard that is still highly adopted. The Net Promoter System (NPS) was created in 1993—before Google, before Netflix and before Microsoft Windows—and has become today's most widely adopted measurement standard for customer experience. However, I am neither a promoter, nor a detractor of the NPS question (a little NPS humor).

It is a good method for benchmarking performance, assuming that the groups being benchmarked are using the same methods, wording, graphics, and request timing to collect the NPS feedback. To drive that point home, using the same question doesn't always yield the same results.

1.  Colorizing the questions with red, yellow and green will yield better results than the same question without the colors.

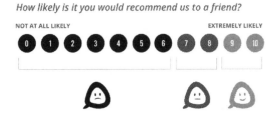

*How likely is it you would recommend us to a friend?*

2.  The timing of the survey will yield different results. For instance, if a car dealer asks a customer the "Likely to Refer" question as they are driving their new car off the lot, they will get better results than asking the same question a week later, when the new car smell is wearing off and the customer still can't figure out how to connect their phone with Bluetooth.

3.  The front-line person interacting with the customer can impact the results. If an employee discusses the survey with the customer and persuades them to complete it, this level of engagement will yield both higher completion rates and higher scores.

NPS is an average qualitative measurement tool. Assuming the representative sample is large enough, the responses can be used for process or product improvement.

We conducted a side-by-side comparison of NPS and an "overall satisfaction" question. In the question, we asked customers to self-report with "Great Experience," "Just OK," or "Unpleasant Experience" options. We asked customers both questions and received over 200,000 responses. One interesting data point is that over 2.5% of the respondents reported that they had a great experience, but answered eight on the "likely to refer" question, making them passive on that scale.

The biggest decline was the sixes. Just over 10% of the test group selected that they had an "OK Experience", but answered the NPS question with a six. While we offer the NPS question to customers, we are not passionate about it either way. It only fits into the plan if it is important to the business for benchmarking or to measure against a previous data set. It can be fun to watch your NPS scores improve month over month as you evolve your CX strategy.

Think about it like this—the NPS question doesn't tell Jill, your counter agent in Denver, anything about her personal service in real-time. You may be able to use your point of sale and figure out who was working that day at that time and create an employee level report, but the question doesn't ask if the customer would refer based on their interaction with Jill. Instead, it asks if the customer is likely to refer. By the time Jill sees her scores (if ever), the data has aged and usually has been sitting in a report for days, weeks or months. In this case, it will have little to no impact in Jill's behavior.

## Overall Satisfaction

## NPS Question

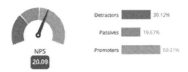

NPS is said to be a great predictor of growth. This means that if you have bad NPS scores then your customers are not happy and you probably have products, people and processes to fix. If you have great scores, your customers are happy and they'll be back—and may bring their friends. Additionally, you can parse their comments and likely figure out where to focus your improvement. I agree that NPS is definitely a predictor of growth. But, the word "predict" is where I get twisted up—to predict is to estimate what will happen in the future. I predict LSU, Alabama, Clemson, or Ohio State will win the next College Football National Championship. Like my brilliant observation about the 2020 football season, NPS feedback can be pretty good at telling us what we already know.

Whether or not NPS is a good predictor of growth is not the right question. The right question is, "Is NPS a great DRIVER of growth?" The answer is, not really. If you are measuring the NPS of a product, then the comments will offer some good insights for improvement. If the measurement is about a service that is impacted by an employee, then the employees knowing that the survey is being sent may cause improved behavior and customer experiences. Also, seeing monthly reporting can make service levels more top-of-mind for employees. But NPS isn't intended to measure individual interactions or experiences. The magic happens when survey questions are specifically about a client's interaction with an individual employee, and the responses are put into motion to drive improvement in real time.

Below is a brief history of the NPS question and the NPS scoring model. It is worth mentioning that in part, I owe my job to Fred and this question. In the evolution of customer experience management, NPS played and continues to play a big role.

### The Origin of NPS

In 2003, Fred Reichheld[1] of Bain & Company launched a project to find a better way of measuring how well an organization treats customers and generates loyal relationships, working with data supplied by Satmetrix. The result was the Net Promoter Score: a metric said to predict customer purchase and referral behavior. Reichheld shared the methodology so anyone could apply it, and NPS became widely adopted by companies to gather customer feedback.

It was determined that the strongest sign of customer loyalty is measured by customers who are happy enough to recommend a product/service to a friend. Reichheld said that when customers act as references, they put their own reputations on the line, and will do so only if they feel intense loyalty.

After NPS was refined, Reichheld released an article in the *Harvard Business Review* that laid out the value of NPS to businesses. It explained how NPS frames the question around how likely customers are to recommend a company in general, as well as how to calculate a score indicating

---

[1] Fred Reichheld is a best-selling author, speaker and business strategist. He is the creator of the Net Promoter System of management.

potential for growth through retention and word-of-mouth.

## The Question

NPS is different from other metrics because it does not measure a customer's satisfaction with a specific interaction. Rather, NPS is designed to measure a customer's overall loyalty to the brand regarding repeat purchases and referrals.

NPS does this by asking a single question, determined to be applicable for most industries: "How likely are you to recommend [This Company] to a friend or colleague?" The customer is then prompted to give a score between 0 and 10, used to calculate the company's Net Promoter Score.

According to Reichheld's scale, 10 means "extremely likely" to recommend and zero means "not at all likely." When examining the customer behaviors along this scale, three clusters were defined:

**"Promoters" gave ratings of 9 or 10,** considered a powerful asset. They're customers with the highest rates of repurchases and referrals, likely to actively recommend your company to others. In most cases, the respondent is also asked to leave comments about their answer.

**"Passives" logged a 7 or 8,** meaning they will likely not hurt or help the business. Because they are only somewhat satisfied, but not enthusiastically loyal, they are not likely to actively recommend your company to others.

**"Detractors" scored from 0 to 6,** indicating dissatisfaction with your company. These are people who will not only discourage or abstain from referring friends, family, and colleagues to a business, but may even seek to do damage to a company's reputation due to their unhappiness. In a sense, every detractor represents a missed opportunity to add a promoter to the customer population—one more unpaid salesperson to market and generate growth on your behalf.

### How to Calculate

The actual Net Promoter Score is then calculated by taking the percentage of promoters and subtracting the percentage of detractors. Passive responders are not used in this final calculation, because they don't influence a potential new customer's decisions one way or the other.

This will generate a score ranging from -100 to 100. A positive NPS means that you have more people recommending your company or product organically than discouraging others from it. A negative score would mean the opposite. Scores higher than 0 are typically considered to be good and scores above 50 are considered to be excellent.

For example, if you surveyed 100 customers and 70% were promoters, 20% were passives and 10% were detractors, your NPS score would be 60 (70 - 10 = 60).

## What's Your Favorite Company's NPS?

### Facebook: NPS of -21[2]

Facebook's score is just ugly. While NPS is considered an indicator of satisfaction and loyalty, it may not be the best tool for a product with over 2 billion users.

According to Gibson Biddle, a former executive at Netflix and Chegg, Facebook is considered to be a communication utility, and people don't tend to rave about utilities as much as other products/services. He also notes that some reports suggest Facebook has plenty of detractors due to privacy issues.

### Zappos: NPS of 57[3]

Online retail company Zappos is well-known for their culture and company values, one of which is "Build Open and Honest Relationships with Communication." Zappos uses the Net Promoter Score drawn from customer surveys to measure customer service performance, and also created the Happiness Experience Form based on how well the agent fulfilled the following:

---

[2] https://customer.guru/net-promoter-score/facebook
[3] https://customer.guru/net-promoter-score/zappos-com

- Tried to make a personal emotional connection
- Maintained their rapport and received a positive customer response
- Addressed the unstated needs of the customer
- Gave a "WOW" experience or went above and beyond what was expected of them

**Starbucks: NPS of 77**

Starbucks survey receipts used to offer one dollar off your next purchase or be worth one free tall hand-crafted beverage. Today, in-store surveys are a thing of the past, as Starbucks now sends emails to rewards members asking them to rate recent visits. This used to be in exchange for bonus stars, but changed in 2019 to offering no incentive at all.

NPS doesn't measure specific interactions. NPS is designed to measure a customer's overall loyalty to the brand regarding repeat purchases and referrals, not a customer's satisfaction with a specific interaction. For executives in the experience space, we are mapping journeys and interactions within journeys. We are searching for meaningful improvement as we go. The interactions are where we see the biggest lift in business outcomes and that is where the CX 2.0 magic happens.

To recommend or not to recommend? That is the question (a little *Hamlet* humor).

## CX Tribe

Adding NPS to your strategy is not a bad idea, depending on the campaign. It is especially useful if you have used it previously and already have a "before" data set. A proper CX 2.0 strategy will create measurable NPS score improvements. How important is NPS to your organization? How important is the reporting and benchmarking to your executives? How do you ask the NPS questions? When do you ask it? Is it automated? If NPS is important, then add it to your strategy.

Now, let's make a shift from the old to the new—from data at rest to data in motion—and learn how to drive great business outcomes with automation.

CHAPTER SIX

# The CX 2.0 Shift

**N**o more box-checking solutions. No more siloed technologies. No more parking an unhappy customer in a report for some executive to look at later. No more "Data at Rest" waiting for someone to react to it.

Instead, design a strategy that puts "Data in Motion" to drive business outcomes. This is the important CX 2.0 shift—from data-at-rest sitting in a report waiting for someone to read and react—to data-in-motion, driving improvement.

**If the customer is a promoter, then use them for promotion via automation.**

Put your data in real-time motion to drive behavior and business outcomes. Maximize the search benefits wherever possible. If someone loves the service provided, collect the feedback and share it on social media, on company websites and other third-party review sites with automation. This makes a promoter an actual promoter. It will create new business and can be used as a backlink-building exercise to drive SEO traffic to your websites and through your marketing funnels.

**If the customer is a detractor, fix it now and make them a promoter.**

Often, the most powerful promoter was once a detractor. If feedback is unfavorable, quickly apologize to the customer and escalate the issue to management. Have a customer care representative, a manager, or an executive reach out to them within minutes of receiving their feedback. Resolve the customer's issue right then and there to create another promoter. This will give brilliant insights into the customer journey, create quality processes and improve customer retention, employee training and behavior.

*"Your most **unhappy customers** are your greatest source of learning"*
*- BILL GATES*

**Customer feedback should be automated.**

Collect and share the customer's honest feedback. When possible, ask a question or two about the quality of service from the front-line employee. Use these questions to give each front-line employee a CX score to be added as a component to the employee's compensation to drive employee behavior. Engage your employees by creating some fun competitions and annual customer satisfaction leader awards. Responses to the questions should provide real-time improvement in employee behavior and customer experience without needing any manual intervention.

Now you are ready to design a CX 2.0 strategy for your business. If you have a lot of siloed, disconnected technologies, you may need to start with less than the entire puzzle. You will get there, provided that you follow the rules and create a Virtuous Cycle that drives business outcomes. Here is a list of the rules that shift us from **Data at Rest** to **Data in Motion,** driving business improvement outcomes. In the next nine chapters, we will describe each rule in detail and share some stories learned along the way. For now, here's a brief rundown.

# 1

# FOCUS ON THE MOST IMPACTFUL INTERACTIONS

# 2

# START WITH
# BEHAVIOR

# 3

# KNOW AND DRIVE BUSINESS OUTCOMES

# 4

# WHEREVER POSSIBLE, AUTOMATE

# 5

# ESCALATE
# AND RESOLVE
# ISSUES

# 6

# MANAGE
# CONTENT AND
# CONSISTENT
# DATA

# 7

# COLLECT
# AND SHARE
# FEEDBACK

# 8

# CREATE A VIRTUOUS CYCLE

# 9

# MAKE DATA-DRIVEN DECISIONS

## CX Tribe

Following the nine rules will drive many great business outcomes. In each chapter, design your outcomes, automation, scorecards and then test your designs against the rules. Develop a list of the questions and fears that come to mind. These are going to prove important as your understanding continues to develop. Don't just read. Be sure to design and test against the rules.

Now let's get your designs started with a very basic journey mapping exercise…

CHAPTER SEVEN

# Rule #1: Focus on the Most Impactful Interactions

I n preparation for this book, I have spent years studying, writing, developing, presenting, debating, and selling CX. I have had the opportunity to learn from hundreds of marketing and CX professionals. Many experts have shared stories where experience data was turned into actionable intelligence that saved and/or earned their companies tens of millions of dollars. In this chapter, we will focus on the story that caused me to add the rule "Focus on the Most Impactful Interactions." As we have already discussed, this book focuses primarily on building CX strategies to drive behavior and power business outcomes. But, as my friend and CX star Erin Clark pointed out, not all interactions are created equal.

Last year, I was in Boston visiting the Horace Mann and Clearsurance leadership teams. Erin Clark is the VP of Experience at Horace Mann, an insurance company with a mission to help all educators protect what they have today and prepare for a successful tomorrow. They have an awesome story, and much of our time together was focused on designing strategies to help Horace Mann collect and share the voice of their customers. Who better to tell those experiences than the ones whose lives have been impacted most by Horace Mann initiatives?

When we met, Erin stood at the white board, dry erase marker in hand, and began talking about customer journeys. She drew circles representing the different journeys, with additional shapes under each journey representing interactions.

Erin explained that most industries have about 10 seminal journeys—the ones that really matter to drive business outcomes. Each of these journeys have multiple interactions. If we assume that there are 5 - 10 interactions within each journey, you must fixate on those that are most impactful. For Horace Mann, Erin highlighted the human interactions where behavioral improvement would power the desired business outcomes.

1.  **Local Agent Experience** – Focusing on Horace Mann agents' direct relationships and interactions with educators and their families is the perfect starting point. The company encourages their agents to be partners for improvement in the educator communities they serve. They strive to make an impact at the local level, and want to get the word out. This can be done by collecting and sharing the voice of the educator, everywhere. The impact of this campaign would be big: helping to grow the local agent's top-line revenue and improve the Horace Mann brand and culture almost instantly.

2.  **Claims Experience** – A campaign that measures and drives great claims experiences is the ultimate fulfillment of the company's promise to their customers. In this example, we could measure the claims interactions, as well as rank and reward adjusters for ease of communication, professionalism and expedience to restore life

to normalcy. The visibility and accountability this campaign would create for adjusters could change their behavior and get people back into their cars and homes faster after damage. It would give Horace Mann leadership better visibility into the quality of their adjustor workforce, their processes and their network of appraisers, body shops, and local contractors.

3.  **Employee Experience** – In my brief experience with Horace Mann there is one thing I can say for certain: the employees I have interacted with are extremely passionate about their jobs. Erin lights up when she tells the Horace Mann story. There are roughly 3,000 company employees and agents, and those I spoke with are big believers in the company mission. Periodically collecting employee feedback and asking employees to share their stories on sites like Glassdoor and Indeed would give Horace Mann brilliant insights from the field, a win for their recruiting initiative to find talent that shares their passion, and a big culture boost.

These three interactions definitely fit in the "Impactful Interactions" bucket. They will all have a measurable, positive impact on the business. But what about the other customer journeys? What about when someone goes to the website for an automated quote?

If Horace Mann isn't paying attention to CX here, it could cost them. See that phone number on the image above? How's the experience when contacting support? Live chat? Payment processing? Roadside assistance?

Erin and her team have a massive job. If there are server lags, redirects, browser incompatibilities, or any number of other issues, they could lose a customer's attention, and the opportunity to win their business. The team needs to not only understand customer interactions, but determine which ones are the most important. This is what they should do:

1. Map journeys and interactions to business outcomes
2. Identify human-to-human interactions
3. Focus on the most impactful interactions

## Map Journeys and Interactions

Less is more! If you have mapped 100 customer journeys, you have mapped too many. Unless your job is "Head of Journey Mapping," try not to turn this exercise into a labor of love. Things change quickly and you need to be agile.

Take Horace Mann. Their team has a massive number of customer-facing journeys. We didn't even get into employee and agent journeys like recruiting, boarding, training, personal development, continuing education, annual reviews or off-boarding interactions. But by mapping journeys and interactions to business outcomes, Erin is confident they are focused on the most impactful journeys.

Here are the basics for mapping a single journey:

1. Set the customer objectives for the journey
2. Profile the personas and define their goals
3. List all the interactions within the journey
4. Identify the best measurement method for each interaction

5. Select the elements you want to show
6. Take the customer journey yourself
7. Build a framework/plan for needed changes

## Identify Human-to-Human Interactions

Do you have a counter agent interacting with a customer? What about a licensed professional selling to or serving a customer? In the Horace Mann example they have adjusters working directly with customers who have experienced a loss. These are human interactions.

## Focus on the Most Impactful Interactions

A customer walking into an insurance office and interacting with a front desk administrative assistant is a human-to-human interaction, but a CX strategy focusing on this interaction won't really move the needle for the company. An insurance company can get the biggest lift from an agent campaign focused on improving the quality of the agent experience.

Start with the most impactful interactions.

## CX Tribe

Don't make your journey mapping exercise a labor of love. Simplify it by choosing a few seminal journeys and focusing on the most impactful. How many journeys have you mapped? How many include impactful human interactions?

Next, let's put review data in motion to drive good business outcomes by starting with behavior.

CHAPTER EIGHT

# Rule #2: Start with Behavior

The reputation management category has grown to hundreds of software companies checking boxes. That will change. Many will go out of business, others will get acquired. A few will stay focused on the needs of a single business vertical. But a couple will become big companies. The next Salesforce will emerge from one of these companies—that is, unless Salesforce is paying attention and buys the winner at just the right moment.

To be clear, the category will not be reputation. The category is experience and will integrate and automate many business systems.

However, businesses move slowly. It won't happen overnight. The companies that remain will look similar, but will execute differently based on a single key factor—the ability to drive engagement and behavior with automation. In the end, the winners will all have a comprehensive platform including reputation, employee engagement, search optimization, reviews, listings, websites, marketing, compliance, AI, and more.

What the winners will not have in common is their primary focus. This will be either behavior or AI. They will all tout both and this will certainly confuse the market. But behavior is everything.

I was recently speaking with the CEO of a well-known reputation management company. He and I had met several times at our church in northern California, but had no clue we were competitors. I later found out that our children knew each other and went to school together. Let's call him Joe. When we spoke, we were talking about the future of the category and our respective companies' growth and direction. Joe is a genius at growing companies, and his current company will be no different. When the mud clears, they will be one of the winners.

During our conversation, we discussed something I had heard one of his executives say at a conference. He told attendees, "We help companies get found, get chosen, and **get better.**" I love the simplicity of the messaging. Honestly, it is brilliant. But, I think it has one major problem—it is out of order. That one signal tells us which direction his company is likely headed.

It's all about where they put the "**get better.**"

I believe it should be, "We help you **get better**, get found and get chosen." That is an important difference. In the version the executive shared, we help you:

1. **Get found** – Share consistent business location data across hundreds of online directories (listings management)

2. **Get chosen** – Help you generate enough reviews to rank higher than your competitors

3. **Get better** – Give you great business intelligence reporting, likely in the form of AI or sentiment

analysis so you can make good decisions and improve your business.

The alternative method, "We help you **get better**, get found, and get chosen" is very different. It says, we help you:

1. **Get better** – Gamify employee behavior through automation to create better customer experiences and drive business improvement

2. **Get found** – Share consistent business location data across hundreds of online directories (listings management)

3. **Get chosen** – Help you generate enough reviews to rank higher than your competitors.

Technically, "get better" goes at the beginning and the end. Behavior powers better experiences and a lot more data. Putting your "get better" first is the bedrock of a great CX 2.0 strategy, and it works time and again. Systems that put "get better" first are going to WOW you and your customers while driving great business outcomes with an almost instant impact on the entire business.

A company should not have to react to the data or read a report to "get better." Most of what they will find in those reports are things they already know. If the lines at the rental car counter are long, you certainly already know you need more staff for peak times. A good strategy will give you data you don't know, and will improve itself, quickly.

### *The data will improve the data.*

Imagine you are the CX lead at Plumb-It, a big national plumbing business. This company creates thousands of customers weekly and works primarily with contractors. I imagine they have a hard time managing their reputation and controlling customer experiences through thousands of contract plumbers in the field.

Through the first filter, Joe's company would help them get found by managing their listings and citations everywhere. They would help them get chosen by getting local customers to write reviews on Google My Business and other relevant sites to help them rank higher in search, specifically Google local search. And they would help them get better by giving them great business intelligence and reporting.

In this scenario, Plumb-It would see a big improvement in leads and top line revenue. They would likely have a

10 - 12% survey response rate. They would know that the contractors aren't showing up on time and don't always clean up after themselves. Just knowing the company is sending review requests to every customer would improve contractor behavior and create an increase in scores, loyalty and other relevant contractor behaviors.

All in all this is a fantastic result. Plumb-It should call Joe and his company immediately. Those are all great outcomes. Now, take the same story through the CX 2.0 example and move behavior to the front of the line.

Plumb-It develops a strategy that starts with a focus on gamifying the right behavior. They start by thinking about Jack, a plumber in Macon, Georgia. Here is a list of some of the business outcomes they want to drive with their strategy:

> **Improve customer experiences** – Their online reputation has created a lot of friction for their company brand and culture. Plumbers not communicating and not showing up on time are the biggest complaints they receive. Therefore, they hope to drive...
>
> • Improved customer communications
> • Plumbers arriving at the customer's home

within the promised service window with fewer reschedules
- Plumbers cleaning up after the job

**Improved customer contact information –** The company has found it extremely difficult to get plumbers to update the address, email and telephone numbers for the customers. That's good data, which could be powerful for marketing and loyalty programs.

**Urgency to close tickets** – Plumbers often wait until the end of the day or the next morning to update the system notes, job complexity, reschedules and closing of the service tickets. Distributing jobs to plumbers with the best customer satisfaction would greatly improve call center communication with the customer. It would also improve survey delivery and response rates.

**More online reviews and social proof** – When you find them online, you mostly see unhappy customer reviews. Not managing the online conversation is causing them to lose business. Getting their happy customer to tell their stories online would be big for creating top line revenues.

**Reward top performers and prioritize job distribution** – Passing out jobs is usually done by proximity and availability. Distributing jobs to the best performers in customer satisfaction would have a big impact on behavior and customer experience.

While there are potentially many more, let's stop there. Plumb-It starts by creating a plumber scorecard and survey. The scorecard includes:

**Response rates** – Engagement

**Bounce rates** – Data quality

**Ticket data** – Same day ticket updated and/or closed

**The survey includes questions about...**
- Communication
- Timeliness
- Cleanliness
- Satisfaction with the work performed
- Likeliness to refer

**A secondary workflow asks customers to write a review on the local Google My Business account for Plumb-It**

**Area, Region and National Rankings** – Each time a new review is entered and a plumber is scored/ranked based on the items above, the scoring model updates accordingly

After the strategy is deployed, Jack is given an assignment by the Plumb-It team. He knows that a significant percentage of his income is based on his scorecard and logs in daily to see how he compares to the other five plumbers in the area. Jack also knows that if he falls below a certain score, he may no longer receive work from Plumb-It, as they now pass out jobs in his area based on his customer satisfaction scorecards. Jack also knows that the district manager gets a notification every time that one of his customers gives a score of under 3 stars. The district manager will likely call the customer right away.

In this example, Plumb-It has built automation that fixes the core issues with behavioral drivers. Jack wants more business from Plumb-It. Jack is in complete control of the outcome. Jack will now get three to four times the reviews compared to other methods. He is now engaged and motivated to deliver great customer experiences through better communication, updating customer data and closing tickets in a timely manner. And Jack's new drive to beat the other plumbers in the area will have a big impact on Plumb-It's local presence on search engines like Google.

Either program would be great for Plumb-It. Although, pushing their "get better" to the front of the line and building behavioral drivers and gamification via qualitative measurement of the individual would yield far superior results.

## Gamification of Customer Satisfaction

As we consult on CX 2.0 strategies for brands today, we focus on four primary behavioral drivers: Ego, Compensation, Competition, and Accountability. We also focus on two types of individuals: the autonomous route-to-market employee and the hourly employee. Finally, we think about each deployment as a campaign built around an interaction. We work to maximize the outcomes from each campaign. Companies most often have multiple campaigns running simultaneously.

Engagement is everything. When you ask your employees to improve NPS scores, they won't be engaged in that outcome. They will likely tell you that they are already doing a great job and the NPS scores are not about them. Instead, create a method for collecting qualitative data at the employee level and update the way you pay employees to include a factor based on their individual scores. Now they will definitely be engaged.

"Get better" doesn't simply come from reading a dashboard, a report or an AI interface. It comes from engaging employees and putting them in control of the outcome.

We call this the behavioral deck of cards. The deck shuffles depending on the situation. In one campaign, ego is the primary driver, in another it's compensation. But in every case, these four will engage employees, create better customer experiences and power business improvement outcomes.

> **Ego** – It feels good when people are appreciative of our hard work. When people say good things about us, it makes us want to do better work every time. If you've ever read Gary Chapman's *Five Love Languages*, then you know about "Words of Affirmation." What you might not know is that "Words of Affirmation" is the most common of the five and is relevant not just in our relationships with our loved ones, but in our everyday lives as well. Many of us

are desperate for affirmation. Our children score a hat trick in the soccer game and still want us to tell them how well they did the second they leave the field. You finish a big project at the office. You know you did amazing work, but it's still not good enough. You need affirmation from your friends and co-workers. Feedback that focuses on individual performance and then alerts the individual on every response will improve customer experience almost immediately.

**Compensation** – If you want people to show up on time, measure and reward them for showing up on time. With the right strategy, compensating staff for delivering great customer experiences always works. If you want them more engaged with the survey, pay them for minimum response rates. You will get higher response rates. If you want to clean up your customer's contact data, put delivery and bounce rates into their scorecard and your data will be nearly perfect.

**Competition** – Winning is fun. When an employee logs into their experience dashboard, the first thing they should see is their results and how they stack up against others doing the same job. If a location manager logs in, they should see how their location and employees are ranking. Companies should offer monthly leader awards and annual top performers awards. Creating fun competition will have a significant impact on motivating employees to do better. Also, it will tell you who your leaders are. They can show their best practices to others. And it will be clear who you may have to let go if they can't or won't improve.

**Accountability** – Send the survey immediately after service delivery. If the customer is upset, escalate it. Call the customer, fix the problem and make them a promoter. This creates better employee behavior, and happier customers.

As you can see, I am a firm believer in driving engagement and behavior into the strategy and making the "get better" an automated piece of the puzzle. Reporting and AI play a big role in the strategy and can help you evolve the strategy to drive other business outcomes. Always build your CX strategy with the outcomes in mind, using automation, and make your "get better" focus the engine, not the caboose, of your CX train.

## CX Tribe

For human interactions, a good CX 2.0 strategy creates a Virtuous Cycle that starts and finishes with targeted behaviors. Think about driving business outcomes for your business at a campaign level. Is there a human interaction that impacts customer satisfaction and loyalty?

Write or type the words "get better" on a design document. Make a list of what that means to you. Maybe your "get better" is about happier employees, happier customers, better data, great reputation, improved marketing and loyalty. What about retention and recruiting? Maybe you just want contractors to show up on time. After you finish this brainstorm, rewrite each item through the filter of the employee behavior that will drive that outcome. For example, change better customer data to: Get agents to update the CRM with better customer contact data within one hour of the service call.

Next, let's create a business improvement framework.

CHAPTER NINE

# Rule #3: Know and Drive Business Outcomes

There is no such thing as perfect execution the first time around. You'll build the strategy, launch it, learn from it, improve it, and expand on it over time. When we built our company, we thought it would be a great tool to collect feedback and share it on social media. That is why we named it "Social" Survey. Luckily, we built it with a full company hierarchy and only accepted full company deployments. Within 12 months, it became evident that it would be way more than a social sharing tool. Customers seem to line up to say, "Since you can do this, can you do that?"

For example...
***"Since you have the employee-level CX data, can you create employee scorecards?"***

From there...
***"Since you have scorecards, can you rank employees in real time against others in their office, region, and the entire company?"***

From there...
***"Can you benchmark the entire industry?"***

From there...
***"Can you develop custom algorithms by industry with things like bounce rates and other relevant data points in the scoring model?"***

From there...
***"Can you ask questions about two different employees that impacted the customer and separate the scores based on their personal questions?"***

And on and on—and this is just about employee scorecards. It seems every part of our system is constantly being challenged to drive more outcomes and bring better results. Setting up the system properly creates great outcomes, which drives even more great outcomes. When you finish this book, you will have the advantage of knowing much of what we've learned and understanding the interconnectivity of seemingly disconnected issues. This should give you a basic understanding of the outcomes you want to drive.

Systems and strategies that put "get better" at the end are going to give you some visibility, while systems that put "get better" first are going to WOW you and your customers with almost instant outcomes that impact your entire business.

Every business is unique. It is a great exercise to write down your story and list out the pain points. It will also be fun to look back at where you started in a year or two. Airbnb is a fantastic example of a company that built a CX program with a focus on driving great business outcomes.

### Airbnb

Both hosts (property owners and managers) and guests (renters) have ratings. I've never read my personal guest reviews, but I do make an effort when I leave an Airbnb to clean everything and start a load of towels. I figure if there is a rating, I want a good one.

Where Airbnb shines is driving behavior of their hosts. In May, I visited Nashville and stayed in an Airbnb. Our company almost always tries to find a great Airbnb instead of booking rooms at the event's host hotel. We find it is usually a better experience, way more cost effective, and has nicer accommodations. Also, we love that it gives us team building opportunities.

To check in at our Nashville Airbnb, we received a welcome email with the lockbox code, directions, internet instructions and methods to easily connect with the host. When we arrived at the rented townhouse, it was immaculate. Nothing was out of place. On the counter was a basket with snacks and a handwritten thank you note. There were water bottles in the fridge. Walking through the house we noticed the closets were stocked with extra towels, sheets, blankets, pillows; even small bottles of lotion, shampoo, conditioner and body wash in the bathrooms.

I have come to expect this level of attention to detail from the homes we book through Airbnb. While we were there, we had an issue with a door locking properly. We called the host to let them know. When we returned to the house after the days events, the issue was resolved and their was a bottle of wine waiting on the counter.

The day we were due to leave the Nashville townhouse I got a call from the host. She wanted to talk about the review request I would receive after checkout. She wanted to make sure that if I was rating less than 5 stars on any of the questions, she could have the opportunity to make it right.

Airbnb asks that you review your stay based on seven key factors in addition to written comments. Guests submit individual star ratings on:

> **Overall experience:** how was the overall experience?

> **Accuracy:** how accurately did the listing page represent the space?

> **Cleanliness:** did the cleanliness match expectations of the space?

> **Arrival:** how smooth was the check-in process, within the control of the host?

**Communication:** how responsive and accessible was the host before and during the stay?

**Location:** how appealing is the neighborhood (safety, convenience, desirability)?

**Value:** did the listing provide good value for the price?

In each category, hosts will have a unique score. I asked the host why this was so important, and she shared that "the rating is everything." Properties with a volume of 5-star reviews usually get gobbled up first over ones with no reviews. Properties with a lot of 5-star reviews are almost never empty and hosts are able to get higher nightly rents. Airbnb can be a big profit center for hosts who win the 5-star competition.

Social proof plays a big role in succeeding on Airbnb. Their CX strategy is driving all the right behaviors, including some pretty fantastic SEO benefits for the Airbnb site. First, hosts know that winning is about reviews, so they focus on great communication, cleanliness, listings accuracy, and a smooth check-in process. Airbnb even added a "Superhost" designation to reward their top performers.

ENTIRE HOUSE

**Charming Victorian**

4 guests · 2 bedrooms · 2 b
Wifi · Kitchen

★ 4.91 (68) · Superhost

## CX 2.0 - Outcomes

Airbnb found a way to manage millions of hosts with a CX strategy. They don't send a 30-question survey, they put data in motion and drive behavior that creates a Virtuous Cycle of great business outcomes. A good CX 2.0 strategy is the perfect intersection for HR, marketing, sales, service, and even compliance. The right strategy has the power to connect the departments through constant WOW moments and documented wins. Many of the minefields they each navigate daily can be cleared with the right strategy.

Airbnb is using a 5-star CX strategy to drive many business outcomes, such as extra towels in the closets. Your business is likely different and will have its own unique list of business outcomes within each of the buckets below:

**HR**

1. Engagement
2. Behavior
3. Recruiting
4. Retention
5. Training
6. Quality
7. Measurement

**Marketing**

8. Content
9. Links
10. Consistent listing data
11. Third-party reviews
12. Social proof
13. Audience building
14. Improve CX
15. SEO
16. Loyalty
17. Marketing programs adoption

**Sales**

18. Grow revenue
19. Conversion
20. Referrals
21. Beating competition
22. Referenceable user stories

23. Improve strategic partnerships
24. Social selling
25. Increase lead volume

**Service**

26. Improve customer data
27. Escalate issues
28. Adoption
29. Training
30. Boarding

**Compliance**

31. Engagement
32. Mentions monitoring
33. Social control and monitoring
34. Reporting
35. Archives
36. Complaint resolution
37. Measurement

Again, your situation is unique. You will have outcomes not listed. Your story defines the problem and helps you get to a list of business improvements you want to drive with automation. The departmental filter may help you identify all the possible improvements and how a good CX 2.0 strategy can power victories across the entire company.

## CX Tribe

HR has an issue with employee engagement and feedback. Recruiting is being negatively impacted by Glassdoor ratings. A customer in Cincinnati is upset about a negative interaction at the counter. Your marketing program's email piece has a terrible open rate. It's all connected. Define your story, list the outcomes, take them through the departmental filter and design your strategy.

Next, let's find out why it is so important to automate everything...

CHAPTER TEN

# Rule #4: Wherever Possible, Automate

W hen our children do something that gets them into trouble at school, we go through a litany of emotions. We know our child is not giving us the entire story, only sharing their perspective. The phrases "That doesn't sound fair," and "I can't believe they would do that" usually find their way into your internal talk track. Then off to the principal's office the next day to fix it. Intuitively we know that in most of these circumstances, we should leave it alone and support the school. We know that consequences of their actions create better behavior in the future. But somehow, consequences for our children hurt us, and our fight instinct is triggered to protect them. If we leave it alone and support the school, there are a lot of great lessons the child can learn. If we fight, they learn another lesson altogether: Mom or Dad will fix it, or that "it's not my fault." It seems nothing is ever their fault.

The same goes for problems within your company—it can, after all, seem like family. Instead of staying out of conflicts most of the time, we often get involved when we shouldn't. Emotional reactions are almost always proportionally incorrect. Designing a highly automated CX strategy is a lot like this. Our instincts to control the outcomes are wrong most of the time.

### Don't Do It

For example, let's say you work at a bank and have been tasked with building a strategy for the bankers on your staff. One of your top earners in Orlando, Steven, decides that he doesn't want his customers to be subject to the survey. "Leave my customers out of it," he says. You don't want to upset Steven, or he might go to another bank. Then your CEO will get angry and want to abandon the entire strategy before you even get it off the ground. So that's it, Steven is out.

Next, Warren, a banker in the same location as Steven, gets a bad review of 2.5 stars. The reviewer commented, "I asked Warren several times to send me materials on the private banking benefits, and I am still waiting. Communication could be better." Now, Warren is unhappy. "That customer has no clue what they are talking about. Either erase that review or remove me from the system!" he shouts. Warren feels entitled to opt out since his colleague Steven already did. You're in a tough spot here. You definitely don't want to upset Warren. You try to reason with him, "It's OK, we will report the review as abusive and get it removed."

Later, Kristin from your Atlanta office comes in with a possible customer review issue. "Today, I had this belligerent customer who decided to go to another bank because they were too stupid to read their disclosures," she says. "How do I prevent them from getting a survey?" You already know that the customer is lost. Sending a survey may just create more friction that you'll have to deal with. You tell Kristin, "Just go into their account and change their email address to donotemail@trashmail.com."

A few weeks later, someone from your tech team comes to you with a request: "We are moving to a new transaction management system. Can you start pulling your survey reports manually and uploading them to the review platform until we figure out the new system?"

That and hundreds of other reasons is how it happens. Human interference creeps in and will corrupt results. You now have no visibility into how Steven is treating his customers. You can't optimize his website or get his customers to leave their feedback on Google. Steven is out, and is already affecting adoption of the other bankers in his office.

Warren now knows how to remove bad reviews when he gets them. He can manipulate the rankings so he will likely win any customer satisfaction competition, just by removing the bad reviews, not by providing better service. Kristin also knows how to manipulate the results. You succeeded at driving Steven, Warren, and Kristin's behavior. However, it's bad behavior that has been reinforced, and the business outcomes will definitely not be the same.

In this example, all bankers from all locations need to be a part of the system. It needs to be a bank requirement that every customer gets the same request. Never allow the option to "opt out."

## Automated Processes

Automation maximizes results. Manual processes minimize results. The example above just illustrated not only employee manipulation, but also the tech team punting on the automated connection. This is a big roadblock in the primary driver of campaign success—the data. Here is a list of the things that need to be automated, as well as places where manual processes make sense:

1. **Transaction Data Integrations (Point of Survey)** – The interaction that you are measuring should be measured as close to real-time as possible, pulled from your transaction management system. The perfect integration would be an API connection that automatically sends requests within minutes of the transaction's completion. The next best integration would be one that pulled data hourly, daily, or twice-a-day. When you do this more than just daily, you start to impact results and response rates. Frontline employees also really appreciate the prompt feedback from their customers.

2. **Review Requests** – Never allow employees to decide which customers they want to review. You want and need the good and the bad. Often, the most valuable outcomes surface from interactions

with unhappy customers.

3.  **Social Sharing** – Sharing reviews on social media sites like Facebook, Twitter and LinkedIn can be automated via APIs and will drive new business. Also, sharing can be throttled if there are too many posts on an account.

4.  **Third-Party Sharing** – Where possible, integrate with relevant websites and share the review data. What sites in your industry do consumers trust? Find a way to push data to them automatically via API.

5.  **Secondary and Tertiary Workflows** – Other third-party reviews sites like Google may not allow you to share review data directly so add secondary workflows. Ask all customers to complete reviews on other sites. You can also ask customers to upload photos, connect with you on social media or even ask for a list of referrals as an additional automated workflow.

6.  **Complaint Resolution** – Collecting feedback, apologizing, escalating to management with alerts and integrations, emailing customers and creating

resolution reporting should all be automated. Since service issues come in many different flavors, you will probably need a manual workflow, but automate as much as possible.

7. **Scorecards** – Create real-time scorecards that update and rank employees.

8. **Reporting** – Individual, location, region and company dashboards, rankings, stats and reports can be automatically rendered to drive behavior.

9. **Audience Building and Retargeting** – By using a simple pixel or retargeting code, happy customer audiences can be built automatically. Use these audiences to build further engagement, collect more customer stories, or encourage direct referrals to your brand.

10. **Business Listings** – Even for a single location, it is difficult to update your name, address, phone, website, hours, photos and category information across over 100 online listing sites (Google, BBB, Yahoo, and more). It is nearly impossible to keep them consistent if you have multiple locations. This is a publishing exercise that must be automated for

all locations.

11. **Backlinks** – When you automate sharing, add backlinks into the shares to drive traffic to your websites.

12. **Sites** – The same publishing method used in "Business Listings" above should be used to build location websites on your domain. A single place for updating name, address, phone, website, hours, photos and category information across the internet and your website will make your job much easier.

13. **Monitoring** – Set up automated alerts and monitor the listings for reviews and mentions of your brand, products and people. Thank the happy customers for mentioning your company online, and connect with any disgruntled customer to let them know their voice is being heard.

By now, I assume you are getting the point. Automate everything you can. However, there are things you should do manually, as well:

## Manual Processes

1.  **Complaint Resolution** – When a customer is unhappy, automation should kick in and give them a forum to communicate their displeasure. Within moments of the feedback, someone from your team should have them on the phone resolving their issues.

2.  **Reply** – Reply to reviews. Make it personal. Show empathy and understanding to unhappy customers and encourage them to reach out. Never use canned responses or automated workflows to reply to customer reviews.

3.  **Motivation and Reward** – Mention great customer stories in daily meetings. Offer daily and weekly prizes for customer satisfaction results. Make a deliberate effort to celebrate top performers and locations.

4. **Compensation** – Customer satisfaction scorecards should impact employee compensation. It can be complicated to map the automated scorecards to payroll without manual intervention. And, don't just reward the front-line employees. Find ways to get the support staff involved. It takes a team to deliver great customer experiences.

5. **Marketing** – While you can automate the connection of relevant marketing systems, adding the best user stories as graphic and video marketing pieces adds credibility and increases conversion.

Every business is different, and you may not be able to start with full adoption and/or a complete strategy. But where possible, require that:

1. Every interaction be measured
2. Every relevant employee is a part of the program
3. Every relevant location is included
4. Reviews are never deleted unless they are actually abusive
5. The data connection is automated so it is consistently implemented

## CX Tribe

Automate the data connection to all closed transactions and never allow a real customer review to be deleted. A good strategy is not meant as a benefit only for top employees. It is not meant to collect a sample set of data or be voluntary. Deleting reviews, opting out employees or only surveying a sample of closed transactions will simply minimize the benefits of your CX strategy. Often company policy and regulatory requirements drive 100% adoption within a company. This can be a valuable tool. As marketers, we are most often providers of on-demand value. We love automation, but almost never "require" anything.

Get buy-in from other departments. Compliance needs the data. HR too. Sales will want the reputation and growth benefits. Rally support and eventually mandate parts of the program as company policy. The perfect CX 2.0 strategy is mostly an automated engine.

Next, sometimes your most powerful promoter was once a detractor. How do you turn an unhappy customer into your biggest advocate?

CHAPTER ELEVEN

# Rule #5: Escalate and Resolve Issues

I t is an honor when a customer chooses your company. There is a lot of competition out there and they could have easily picked a number of alternatives, but they chose you. And, if you do your job exceptionally well, they will choose you again. They may even tell their friends to choose you too. Each customer is a great company asset. Whatever you do, do it with pride, excellence and appreciation for those that chose you.

Great customer experiences can be more valuable than any advertising. But what about bad customer experiences? All transactions are not created equal. Some take weeks or months to complete. A few come with too many variables where many things can go wrong. A life insurance policy can require a physical, with blood tests and an EKG—and not all applicants will qualify. A real estate transaction can get competitive and customers can lose their dream home when multiple offers are submitted. A mortgage requires credit, collateral and cash minimums and many buyers will not qualify.

A customer choosing you does not automatically lead to satisfaction at the end of the transaction. The way you handle what happens next is extremely important. As hard as you may try to WOW every customer, unhappy customers are inevitable. Use automation and manual workflows and seek to turn every unhappy customer into a future repeat customer.

## Uber

When you get out of an Uber, your phone asks you to rate the driver from one to five stars. These stars are very important. Uber uses them to drive behavior of both riders and drivers—that's right, we all have a score. My rating as a rider is 4.93. I watch it almost as closely as my credit score.

Don't ask why, but it kind of upsets me that I don't have a 5-star rating. I have started tipping just in case the driver sees the tip before they rate me.

As for drivers, they are bringing water bottles, candy, and every type of charging cord imaginable to make sure they get 5 stars. One driver told me he cleans his car twice daily. Recently, I had an Uber with an iPad Pro set up as a TV, equipped with countless channels. The driver even had a container of chocolates under an armrest. It was an awesome ride!

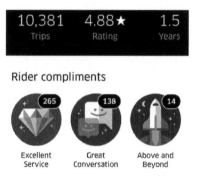

When I order an Uber, I often read the driver reviews before they arrive. Uber uses these reviews to drive behavior, competition, improve experiences, remove bad drivers and resolve customer concerns. Uber is using an automated, immersive strategy to drive great customer experiences and power a lot of business outcomes for their company.

Recently, as I was getting out of an Uber, the driver negotiated a 5-star trade with me. "Of course, but why is this important?" I asked. He went on to explain that if his score drops below a certain score (he said 4.6), then Uber might stop giving him rides all together. In other words, if his score drops below some minimum standard, he could lose 100% of his income. I looked it up online and found this:

> **"You are encouraged to maintain at least a 4.6 average over your most recent 100 trips," Uber tells drivers online. "If your rating over the most recent 100 trips is below 4.6, your profile may be at risk of deactivation."** Jul 25, 2017

My driver had a 4.93 rating with an All-Star driver designation, and had completed more than 10,000 5-star rides, so no risk of this happening. I prodded, "I get it, but that's not a problem for you with a 4.93. Why are you concerned?" He told me that in some major markets like San Francisco, Uber is piloting a method where riders can choose their drivers based on factors like star rating. This made him feel an extreme competitive pressure and he was working hard to get as close to 5 stars as possible. The thought of losing rides to other drivers with higher scores was really impacting his behavior. Uber had this driver so focused on my experience that it was nearly all he wanted to talk about.

As for their level of **C.A.R.E.** (Collect, Apologize, Respond , Escalate), Uber cares so much about your experience that they fix your issues almost instantly when you complain about anything.

A few years back, I was at the College Football National Championship in Arlington, Texas watching Ohio State beat Oregon. After the game, I walked several blocks from the stadium and ordered an Uber. The wait at the stadium was over an hour, but a few blocks away I was able to grab an Uber within minutes. After getting in the Uber, the 10-minute ride to the hotel took over 20 minutes. Not because of traffic, but because the driver missed the exit. As luck would have it, there was no easy way to get back.

After the ride, and the overpriced charge, I found the dispute link on the Uber app and shared that the driver had missed the exit. I told them that it was an accident, but I didn't think I should be charged double because of the mistake, especially since it was surge pricing. Minutes later, I checked the app and had a credit for nearly half of the money back.

Uber makes it easy to connect in app, but they also have a website, help.uber.com, to address nearly any issue. If you get into a smelly car, you can go to help.uber.com and this is what you will find:

## My driver's vehicle was in poor condition

We hope every ride with Uber is safe and comfortable. 5-star partners keep vehicle interiors neat, clean, and free of strong or unpleasant odors.

If the vehicle for this trip truly did not meet expectations of cleanliness or safety please let us know here.

Please use sparingly as complaints can potentially have negative results on driver accounts.

SIGN IN TO GET HELP

Uber is using star ratings to drive accountability that creates better rider experiences. They have a comprehensive and nearly instant complaint resolution process designed to turn detractors into promoters. To be honest, with my rider score and my complaint resolution experiences, I can't remember the last time I opened the Lyft app on my phone. I am an Uber fan.

Like Uber, you should give customers a forum to tell their story and feel like they have been heard. Then, as quickly as possible, fix it. Here are some best practices to follow when designing your strategy.

1. **Collect Feedback** – Unhappy customers need to get their frustrations out. Give them a forum to tell their story. This should be an automated part of the survey workflow. When you know that they had a bad experience, ask them, "Would you tell us what

would have improved your experience?" This puts a positive spin on the question. Do not ask what you did wrong. Instead, ask how you can do better.

2.  **Apologize** – It is true that customers can sometimes be unreasonable. Being upset with your company for things that are unreasonable is not your fault. But that's not the point. They had a bad experience. Apologizing for their bad experience is not an admission of guilt. Simply tell them that you apologize that they had a bad experience.

3.  **Thank them and tell them you hear their concerns** – Thanking someone for leaving negative comments gives them permission to let it go. Make sure they understand that their perspective is important to you. Resist the urge to defend your company, its policies, or your team. Now is not the time to be combative.

4.  **Give them a method to continue the conversation** – Set the expectation that you would like to continue the conversation. If they need to talk about it more, you should want to hear them. Also, talking to you about it may prevent them from

going on social media or third-party review sites.

5.  **Escalate every unhappy customer issue**
    – Within seconds of the negative response,
    someone on your team needs to be alerted to
    the customer's concerns. Likely you will escalate
    to multiple team members. For example, the
    employee's manager, regional director, and the
    customer care/support team.

6.  **Email the customer and reinforce your
    understanding of their concerns** – Have a senior
    manager or someone in customer care email the
    customer. Reinforce that you have heard them,
    their concerns are important and that you'd be
    willing to continue the conversation. Give them a
    method to reach a real person immediately. Avoid
    anything that will amplify their frustration.

7.  **Call every unhappy customer** – If possible, pick
    up the phone and call the customer personally.
    Communicate that you've just received their survey
    response and would like to discuss. Seek to
    resolve their concerns and earn their loyalty.

8. **Track unhappy customer interactions** – Add your comments to reporting and archive all comments, responses and notes. Use these as training tools and opportunities to improve. Many of our clients have told us that while unhappy customers are less than 2% of all responses, they get more value from those responses than the 98% that are over-the-top happy.

9. **Monitor third-party review sites and reply to all unhappy customer feedback** – If someone sees a bad review on Google or another third-party review site, that's not good. Always reply with empathy and understanding, apologize to the customer publicly, and ask them to contact you offline. People who read the review will not only be inclined to ignore the stated infraction, but they may choose your company because of the way you responded to the unhappy customer.

## **Escalation And Resolution Workflows:**
## **American Financial Network**

One of our customers, American Financial Network (AFN) is a great example of best practices for the nine items just listed. Here is how they turn a detractor into a promoter.

**Automated Workflow:** When the customer has an unpleasant experience, AFN responds:

> *We are sorry you had an UNPLEASANT experience. Would you tell us what would have made it better?*

**Automated Workflow:** They collect the customer's response and apologize, tell them their concerns matter, and give them a forum for continuing the conversation. Notice that they offer a conversation with a senior executive:

> *We apologize that you had a bad experience. But, thank you for sharing your concerns with us. In an effort to earn your trust and business in the future, we are going to reach out to you and seek more information. Would you like to speak to one of our senior executives? If so, check your inbox for instructions on how to do that. Your answers to this survey as well as comments you share with our leadership will help us improve the experience of future customers.*

**Automated Workflow:** Next, AFN sends an automated email to the customer to reinforce that they have been heard, that AFN cares about their concerns and offers them a way to escalate the issue further. Here is a copy of that email:

*We are sorry to hear that your recent experience with AFN was less than satisfactory. Our goal is to provide both world-class products and exemplary customer service. We would like to speak with you further to understand where things went wrong and how we might improve going forward. For these reasons, we would like to extend an invitation for you to speak directly with an AFN executive.*

*Please email us at **surveys@afncorp.com** to accept this invitation, and we will gladly set aside time for you to speak with our President, CEO or COO about how we can possibly improve the mortgage experience.*

*Please include your name, phone number and the best time to reach you and you will be contacted by a top-level AFN executive who is interested in your feedback.*

*We appreciate your time and look forward to speaking with you further.*

*Sincerely,*
*The Customer Service Team*
*American Financial Network, Inc.*

**Manual Workflow: Call every unhappy customer** – An AFN executive, often COO Jon Gwin will pick up the phone and call the customer to address their concerns and turn them into a promoter, even if they have taken no action after the initial negative survey.

**Manual Workflow: Track unhappy customer interactions** – While the reporting is automated, after each call Jon or someone from his team takes notes, creates reporting and connects with the original service provider.

**Automated Workflow: Monitor third-party review sites** – AFN monitors the web, specifically Google and Facebook, for unhappy customer reviews and replies to these reviews publicly.

Escalating and resolving customer issues has many positive outcomes. Not every company will be as thorough as AFN. But a good system enables good customer **CARE**: they **C**ollect, **A**pologize, **R**espond, **E**scalate.

# **C**OLLECT
# **A**POLOGIZE
# **R**ESPOND
# **E**SCALATE

**Collect** customer feedback and **apologize** immediately before they exit the survey. **Respond** with an email so the customer has a forum to continue the conversation rather than taking to social media or review sites. **Escalate** the customer's concerns to management and customer care team.

By doing this, you've mitigated online issues, created accountability for your team, given yourself instant visibility into needed improvement, and engaged employees and management in the **CARE** conversation. You've driven behavior that creates better customer experiences.

## CX Tribe

Sometimes, your most powerful promoter was once a detractor. How do you turn an unhappy customer into an advocate? Collect, Apologize, Respond, Escalate (**CARE**). Unhappy customers need to be heard. Even if you give them a forum to leave their concerns, always give them a way (that you control) to continue the conversation.

When a customer is upset with you today, how thorough is your resolution process? Does the unhappy customer feel heard? Is the process you use today manual or highly automated? A good design will integrate into your current workflows and automate much of the process. Create a list of the optimal workflows for your business and begin designing these workflows, emails, texts and notifications.

Next, if you offer great products and services, Google wants to be your friend and refer you business...

CHAPTER TWELVE

# Rule #6: Manage Content and Consistent Data

T hink of Google as a referral partner. Usually a referral partner knows you, your business and trusts that you will do a good job for their friend, family member, or colleague. Google's search ranking methods aren't all that different.

For example, when referring a hair stylist, we know some basic facts:

1. They cut and style hair
2. They have a local business location
3. They are good at what they do

We can attest to their profession and quality of work. Google is similar and accomplishes this through an algorithm that drives both local and organic search results. But to successfully refer customers to your site, Google needs to confirm that you are an actual business, with a real location, that delivers great customer experiences to local customers.

Google's algorithm is looking for the best answer when someone goes online and uses their search engine. The algorithm has great intentions—to find and provide the most relevant, prominent, and local results:

☐ **Relevance**
How accurately a local listing matches what someone is searching for.

☐ **Prominence**
How well-known a business is. This can be based on online information in the form of links, articles and directories.

☐ **Distance**
How far each potential search result is from the location—or Google's knowledge of the location—for the person searching.

### The Google Algorithm

If you are reading this in 2030, all bets are off. In a decade, search intelligence will evolve and likely be focused on a collection of real-time data in partnership with sentiment. I imagine that we will be walking by a restaurant and some device, such as our eye glasses, will show us a video of one of our friends having a great time at that restaurant a few months back. On the same screen we would be able to see how many seats are available, or the expected wait time. It will tell us who the best server is and the date and grade of the last inspection, as well as share three better local options for the same type of food. It might even tell you that you should stay away from spicy food because of the results of your last visit to the doctor.

Let's get back to reality. In 2018, Moz.com published an article titled "Local Search Ranking Factors,"[1] which explained that roughly 81% of Google's local search algorithm centers around the following key factors:

**Google My Business – 25%**

**Link Signals – 16%**

**Review Signals – 15%**

**On-Page Signals – 14%**

**Citation Signals – 11%**

---

[1] https://moz.com/local-search-ranking-factors

A good CX strategy must have automation that drives these five outcomes. Link Signals and Reviews Signals will be discussed in more detail in the next chapter.

### Google My Business

Optimizing your company's locations is crucial for Google to refer local search traffic. With Google My Business (GMB) accounting for roughly 25% of the local search ranking algorithm, every location of a business needs to have a claimed listing with accurate information. If the location can't be found, or if the words "claim this business" appears, then it needs to be claimed—quickly! Linking to GMB and updating the listings data is like saying, "Hey Google, I'm over here."

This is an opportunity to enter complete, accurate data— either by using a service or entering it manually. Thoroughly setting up this information makes it easy for Google to match you with the right searches. Focus on correct name, physical address, local phone number, business category, hours of operation, photos and other attributes.

Here are several tips for optimizing your GMB listings to increase how your business ranks in local search results:

1. **Verify your business location**

   Through an almost unbelievable analog process, Google will send a postcard to your location with a 5-digit number for verification. Manage the Google postcard dance with care, because it looks like an advertisement. Make sure your location managers, marketers and/or administrators know that the Google postcard is being delivered to them via mail and to be on the lookout for its arrival.

2. **Name your location listings to make it easy for Google**

   It helps to put the primary search phrase in your business name (such as ABC Real Estate of Tulsa). Make sure to be consistent with what appears on your website and other sites like Yelp and Bing.

3. **Ensure the address for each location is the same, everywhere**

   If you are at 12677 Alcosta Blvd., Suite 250, then you should be using the exact same address on all of your listings across search engines and directories. If you use "Boulevard" on Yelp, "Blvd." on Google and "Road" on your location's website, you are creating mismatches. Same with suite numbers such as "Suite 250," "Ste 250" and "#250."

4. **Use a local phone number**

   Local phone exchanges usually reinforce that it is a local business. If you have 20 locations that all use the same 1-800 number, then it's clear you have a national call center handling calls for the business.

5. **Use the actual website for each specific branch location**

   When Google crawls the linked site, it should have the local name, address, hours, phone number and other attributes. Try not to link all of your locations to the same web address.

6. **Keep your hours accurate**

   Entering and updating your hours, especially during the holidays, gives both customers and Google more confidence in your business.

7. **Add and update photos and videos regularly**

   Showing your goods and services can help tell the story of your business. Also, photos and videos will most often drive more internet attention on these sites than reviews. If you provide an intangible service, take pictures of happy customers or employees in action—whether that be at work, doing community service projects or at trade shows.

8. **Advanced Users: Use the "same as" property**

   Each business location should have a unique page on your domain and a unique GMB listing. Each page should use the "same as" property on a unique JavaScript Object Notation for Linked Data (JSON-LD) tag. Make sure you have the URL on GMB point to the correct location page, and make sure you have unique content for each account.

9. **Get your customers to write reviews**
   Managing and responding to reviews is extremely powerful.

## On-Page Signals

If a company lists themselves as a mortgage firm in an online directory, but their website says nothing about mortgage, that is a red flag.

I was on a mortgage company's website the other day. It was beautiful, and I could tell they spent a lot of time and money making the sleek design with HD photos and a sophisticated search bar. But there were two problems. First, they did not mention mortgage anywhere on the site, except within the company name. In addition, the phone number they featured did not match the one listed on Google My Business. It looked good, but they did not have rich content alerting Google that they offered what the searcher was looking for.

Websites should make sure they feature high-quality content that tells potential customers about the products and services offered. The process of making sure your website is both user and search engine friendly is referred to as onsite search engine optimization (SEO).

In simple terms, this means adjusting certain elements of your website so that search engines are able to crawl—read your information in order to create entries for an index—and understand the content as well as website structure.

The ultimate goal of onsite SEO is to make it as easy as possible for both users and search engines to:

- Understand what a web page is about
- Identify that page as relevant to a search query by using keyword(s)
- Find that page useful and worthy of ranking well on a search engine results page

There are several ways to be rewarded with high rankings on search engines. One is having sound security and functionality of your site. Check to see if it's mobile-friendly and compatible with all devices and browsers, as well as if the information on your site matches your business listings data.

Consider the content of your site and how relevant it is to

the person searching. What is their intent? Ask yourself this question and create content that is in-depth, unique and trustworthy.

When modifying your site content to make it more crawlable, focus on relevant title and descriptions, creating alternative text for images and incorporating internal links so users stay on your site. All of these combine to create your level of authority on Google. Remember, by improving onsite content and your website's visibility, you are also increasing the quality and quantity of website traffic.

## Citation Signals

A local citation is an online mention of a business's information, commonly known by the acronym NAP (Name, Address and Phone Number). This data can appear on business directories, websites and other social platforms, and is critical for influencing search engines to display local intent.

It can also help internet users discover new, local businesses. For example, say a hungry patron goes on Yelp to find a place for lunch. If a business has accurate citations, the customer may notice the establishment is nearby and can use the number provided to call in and place an order. However, if the business lists inaccurate citations, the customer may be misdirected, leading to a loss of not only revenue, but also reputation.

There are two kinds of citations: structured and unstructured. A **structured** citation is a mention of your business on directories like Yelp and Yellow Pages. An **unstructured** citation is a mention of your business on blogs, news sites and other businesses' pages. Google's algorithm looks at both when ranking search results.

It is important to make sure your business is listed on high authority and industry-specific sites (like Realtor.com for real estate and LendingTree for mortgages) to earn credibility and trust from Google. When defining your citation criteria, focus first on consistency. Next, update sites with authority. Finally, add vertically and geographically-relevant citations. Here's a quick list of sites you should definitely be utilizing:

**Top 15 Citation Sites**

1. Google My Business
2. Bing
3. Facebook
4. Yelp
5. Yahoo
6. Foursquare
7. Apple Maps
8. Express Update
9. Acxiom
10. Factual
11. Localeze
12. Dun & Bradstreet
13. Superpages
14. Citysearch
15. Yellow Pages

Your brand is everywhere—potential customers are finding you on search engines, maps and online directories. A good business listings management and reviews strategy will be well worth your time and effort, helping you win more local business online.

## CX Tribe

Winning on Google with one or 1,000 locations is easy in theory, but complex in practice. Publishing and monitoring consistent location data on over 100 websites for each of your locations is virtually impossible. The bigger you are, the more you will need a listings distribution service to manage this.

Are you familiar with the Google My Business location manager? While you are in the process of setting up your strategy, log in and see how many of your locations are listed. Has your company claimed all its locations?

If you are looking for the secret sauce to winning Google search, this is it. Focus on the things that are important to Google:

1. Google My Business location pages
2. Publish consistent location data everywhere
3. Publish the same NAP data on your website for each location, in addition to rich content about your products and services

Now let's focus on the second half of the Google equation:

4.  Collect and share reviews
5.  Create high quality backlinks driving relevant
    traffic to your domain

CHAPTER THIRTEEN

# Rule #7: Collect and Share Feedback

When designing survey questions, less is more. If your campaign is about a person-to-person interaction, ask questions specifically about that interaction. Make sure the questions promote the right behavior and that the employee can control the outcome. If you ask the customer a question unrelated to the interaction, you will need to leave the answer out of the employee scorecard. Otherwise it will become an excuse for underperformance and seriously hamper the results. If you are trying to drive the behavior of two people who are a part of the same transaction, ask a couple of questions about both of them individually. Keep their scores separate and specific to items that they can control. If your technology can support this, it works well.

We recommend a maximum of six questions. The more questions you ask, the higher the likelihood that the customer will bounce and not finish the survey. Here is an example of a question designed to drive behavior of an individual: "Did [Employee Name] completely explain all of the charges?" In this situation, the company wants to make sure customers understand the charges they will see. Asking this question and incentivizing the results will guarantee improvement and mitigate a lot of problems for the company. If you know the behaviors you want, then you already know what questions to ask.

### Winning on Google

Google loves reviews and so do potential customers. Positive reviews will persuade people to choose your business, and will also have a big impact on search rankings.

Google's crawlers work to deliver the most relevant search results. If their algorithm decides the search term has local intent, they show results in their Local 3-Pack—the map-integrated section that appears just below the pay-per-click results. To get found on Google, your business listings are key. But to win and show up in this 3-Pack for relevant search terms, reviews are extremely important. How you collect, share and reply to reviews on Google, your website, social media, and third-party websites will be impactful and will likely need to be automated to scale.

> **Google Local Search** – As discussed in the last chapter, Google's Local 3-Pack relies primarily on five priorities that must be built into your CX Strategy.

> **Google My Business – 25%**
> **Link Signals – 16%**
> **Review Signals – 15%**
> **On-Page Signals – 14%**
> **Citation Signals – 11%**

### Fusco & Orsini

This morning I did a search for "insurance in San Diego." Not "car insurance" or "homeowners insurance," just "insurance." Online search for insurance is very competitive. Hundreds of companies are fighting for the top spot, especially in a major market like San Diego. Winning on Google can create a lot of new business. If you wanted to buy the keyword "insurance" on Google pay-per-click, it would cost you as much as $48 per click. To own the top spot for "car insurance", it can be more than $100 per click. Ouch!

| Keyword (by relevance) ↓ | Avg. monthly searches | Competition | Ad impression share | Top of page bid (low range) | Top of page bid (high range) |
|---|---|---|---|---|---|
| ☐ insurance | 301,000 | Medium | – | $15.19 | $47.72 |
| Keyword ideas | | | | | |
| ☐ car insurance | 368,000 | High | – | $40.09 | $106.53 |

I also searched for "Insurance Broker, San Diego." Both results were similarly fascinating. One small company with only a few insurance agents found their way to the top of the map integrated local pack—Fusco & Orsini.

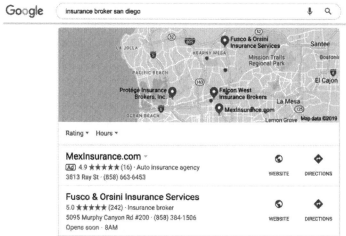

For the "insurance broker" spot, they were #2, only because the #1 spot is an advertisement. For the keyword "insurance," they were #4. There is an ad on this page, as well.

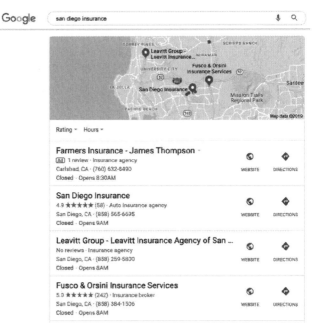

In both cases, they are on Page 1, just below Google's pay-per-click spots. How are they doing it? They have a lot of 5-star reviews. In fact, they have 242 as I'm writing this, and many are very recent. That's 242 local customers who went online and told their story. Google loves it when local customers write reviews for local businesses. This is a signal that the company is doing business locally, and is delivering great products and services. For those of you who live in San Diego and are looking for homeowners insurance—hundreds of your neighbors use Fusco & Orsini and had such a great experience that they went online and told Google about it. Additionally, they wrote comments with the words "homeowners insurance" in them. What does this say to Google? Fusco & Orsini is a **local business (location)**, offering **homeowners insurance (keyword product match)** to local customers who all seem to **love the service (sentiment)**. That's why they are winning. They have turned Google's crawler into a referral partner by doing a great job, updating their business listings and encouraging customers to leave feedback on Google.

Reading Fusco & Orsini's reviews and replies means crawling more than 20,000 words. A flawless 5-star average across 242 reviews is very hard to achieve. There is also positive customer sentiment throughout the reviews. There are hundreds of notable keyword matches. Here are a few of the exact matches found in their reviews:

> Keyword "insurance" used 200+ times
> Keywords "car and auto" used 45 times
> Keyword "home" used 20+ times
> The agents' names used 80+ times

The combination of these components is clearly driving excellent performance online for Fusco & Orsini. It is easy to see why they are winning on Google. For a single office in San Diego, it is not difficult to manage. But for a multi-location brand, it would be virtually impossible to manage. A CX strategy should create and share reviews, where you need them most, via automation.

## Priorities for your CX Campaign

Here is an abbreviated overview for you to consider when building a sharing strategy;

> **Reviews on your Website** – Reviews are like small articles on your website. Collect and aggregate reviews from across the web (Google, Facebook recommendations, other third-party review sites) and host them on your location and company sites. Don't forget to feature the front-line employees and post their reviews on their profile page. Do not use a service that prohibits you from indexing the reviews on your site. Also, avoid linking to a third-party reviews site from your domain. You have potential customers on your website; keep them there.

> **Reviews on Google** – Google My Business has become the most important destination for reviews. Run a workflow that asks every customer to write a Google review. Direct the customers to write reviews on the GMB page for the location. This will create local search optimization and new business. NEVER try gating with Google reviews. Gating is the practice of only asking happy customers to write reviews on Google. This is a violation of Google's Terms of Service[1] and might result in the loss of most, if not all your reviews. Even if you

---

[1] http://bit.ly/CX20_Google

have separate workflows for happy and unhappy customers (as you should), ask both to leave a Google review.

**Reviews on Social Media** – Share your reviews on Facebook, Twitter, LinkedIn, Instagram and other social sites. Always add a link back to your websites where more reviews are hosted. We constantly hear success stories about social posts creating new relationships and business.

**Reviews on Third-Party Websites** – Depending on your business vertical, you likely will have a primary and secondary focus for directing reviews. For real estate agents, it's Realtor.com and Zillow. For mortgage loan officers, it's Zillow and LendingTree. For doctors, it's Zocdoc, Vitals and Healthgrades. Most third-party review pages will offer a feed so you can map the reviews back to your websites. The more important the third-party site, the more priority you should give it within your CX automation.

**Replying to Reviews** – Replying to reviews tells readers that you care. It humanizes the conversation and engages new potential customers. Always reply publicly to negative reviews. Tell them you are sorry they had a bad experience and give them a method for contacting you to discuss. Never be argumentative. No matter how much you want to tell your side of the story, don't.

**Links** – When you share reviews on third-party websites and social media sites, add links back to your websites. Getting links from high-quality websites will seriously boost your page rank.

It is important to emphasize that even if Google didn't reward inbound links and reviews, it would still be a great strategy for growing business. Getting links and reviews and driving traffic from a trusted website to you is simply good business practice. Sharing the true voice of your customer all over social media in front of friends, family and colleagues helps drive more traffic and referrals. It's a smart and inexpensive way to grow your business.

## CX Tribe

Most professionals still get a majority of their business from referrals. An automated online review system is like a referral engine. The same happy customer that would refer a business through word-of-mouth puts their referral out into the world for anyone to see. As you read positive reviews, you are being referred to use the company. If this were the only benefit to collecting and sharing customer feedback, it would be enough. However, it is not the only benefit. Google's crawlers look at links and reviews to create a scoring model that assigns authority. Getting found online is done through consistent data on listings and citations. Ranking higher in search and beating your competitors so you can get chosen is achieved by properly collecting and sharing the voice of your customers, everywhere.

Next, a Virtuous Cycle is a chain of events in which one great occurrence leads to another, which further promotes the first occurrence and so on. If you design your CX strategy to create a Virtuous Cycle, every win leads to more wins.

CHAPTER FOURTEEN

# Rule #8: Create a Virtuous Cycle

In every circumstance, your CX 2.0 strategy should create a "Virtuous Cycle." This is a chain of events where one desirable occurrence leads to an even more desirable outcome, further promoting the first occurrence and creating a continuous process of improvement. If you think about driving behaviors and business outcomes without the filter of the Virtuous Cycle, you would likely miss the leverage and power in the connectivity of the parts. This is a powerful workflow "muscle" that needs to be developed. For most of us we need to develop the "and then what?" muscle. When I had a conversation about one of our hospitality clients with

Brittany Hodak, a keynote speaker who teaches business leaders to multiply customers by creating superfans, we discussed this very "muscle."

Brittany is the co-founder of The Superfan Company, an organization that creates more loyal customers by harnessing the power of fandom. She's spearheaded assignments for Walmart, Katy Perry, Unilever, Amazon, Taylor Swift, and Johnson & Johnson, just to name a few. I am a superfan of Brittany, and I understand why big brands call on her. She understands the connectivity of the customer journey and designs creative strategies to help them out.

The particular client we were discussing was seeing big improvements in their customer data, NPS scores, customer engagement and online reputation. After hearing about their progress, Brittany said, "OK, then what did you do?" I said, "What do you mean?" She continued, "Do they have a rewards program? Can you add a question to the workflow asking customers if you can automatically add them to the rewards program and give them a free day on their next rental?" After this conversation we immediately began work to include this workflow to automate loyalty program membership.

To her point, we have great customer contact data. We know which customers are happy. And at that moment when they are finishing the survey, we have their attention. Why not drive another business outcome, such as loyalty? Within seconds Brittany connected the three successes to the loyalty outcome. If you are not thinking about your CX strategy like a Virtuous Cycle, you would likely miss this.

In this situation, **Improved Employee Behavior** leads to **Better Customer Experiences** and **Data.** Happier customers are more engaged and willing to leave feedback at scale, which can be shared to **Power Online Reputation.** Happy customers can be added to custom audiences, retargeted, and added to rewards programs to **Improve Marketing and Loyalty Outcomes.** Happy, more engaged customers always lead to happier employees, which will greatly **Improve Recruiting and Retention Outcomes.** Finally, happier employees deliver great service and start the cycle again, and again, and again.

Every business is different. But remember, people are people. CX 2.0 most often focuses on behaviors that drive people. It measures, rewards and improves people. What behaviors do you want to encourage in your people to get the desired outcomes?

Start with behavior and end with behavior. When designing your strategy, focus on being automated, immersive and creating a Virtuous Cycle.

Here are some examples of behavior cycle starters for various industries:

> **Call Centers** – If you want your customer care teams to drive more one-touch resolutions, then create a strategy that drives that behavior through compensation and competition workflows where the scoring model weighs one-touch resolutions more heavily. More one-touch resolutions create better customer experiences, more 5-star reviews, a well-trained staff, and so on.

**Software Companies** – If you want to cut your boarding times in half, create a scoring model that has star rating (quality), completion rate (engagement), and days to board as variables. This will drive quicker boarding times and adoption, which could improve customer excitement and engagement, and other great outcomes.

**Restaurants** – If you want your servers to get customer contact information, or loyalty program adoption, or sell more desserts, or collect more 5-star Yelp reviews, or all of these things—measure it at the server level, and reward the right behaviors. Most servers work for tips. That is their best form of feedback. But, management decides who gets the best shifts and sections. Distribute these based upon survey completion rates and scores. Everybody wins.

**Pharmacies** – If you want the pharmacist to come out from behind the counter and build relationships with the customers to combat the market penetration that the mail order pharmacies are driving, then measure, encourage and reward these behaviors. This would have a big impact on customer retention, brand and even company culture.

## CX Tribe

Strengthen your "and then what?" muscle by thinking about your CX strategy as a Virtuous Cycle. There is tremendous leverage and power in the connectivity of the parts. Remember, it is all a single puzzle. This is your opportunity to piece it together.

All of your hard work should result in a lot of great business outcomes and a ton of new information. What do you do with all that CX data?

CHAPTER FIFTEEN

# Rule #9: Make Data-Driven Decisions

With a good CX strategy you will have a lot of data to analyze. There are brilliant insights found in reviews, transcribed calls, chat sessions, social interactions, and Q&A forums. The more your team actively engages in these, the more data you will have. Additionally, a typical CX 2.0 strategy can give you 2-5x the response rates from customers. Even more CX data! What should you do with all of this data? The good news is that you will already be creating a lot of business improvement outcomes. But, this is no excuse to ignore the power of the data. It can create opportunity as well as make and save you millions.

I recently spoke at a CX conference and had the opportunity to meet professionals from some of America's most well-known brands. During these conversations, I heard several stories about major shifts companies made by analyzing CX data. Two of my favorite stories came from Hunter Douglas and a global athletic apparel company. Both companies had partnered with Topbox. This omni-channel conversation analytics firm helps enterprise customers collect and activate insights from every conversation about the company (i.e. mentions, reviews, social) and every conversation the company has with clients or customers (i.e. calls, chat). The two stories below underline how important it is to properly aggregate, analyze and react to the data across all channels.

### Apparel Manufacturer

Christopher Stark joined a leading athletic apparel manufacturer in 2013 as a data analyst, and when he left in 2018 he was the director of the planning analytics team. While there, Chris launched their Voice of the Customer (VOC) program. His team collected and analyzed data from chat, support, product reviews, in-app communications, and social media to extract insights. The biggest problem wasn't how to extract impactful data to improve the business— there were more than enough useful insights. It was how to effectively communicate it, so that internal stakeholders could take action. Chris and his team tried writing and distributing an "Insights" newsletter. They wanted everyone to see all the great findings and get busy improving their respective departments. Unfortunately there was very little engagement, likely because the newsletter highlighted an overwhelming amount of data. Eventually, they evolved their methods to support one valuable insight at a time in partnership with a single department/stakeholder. They would dedicate weeks to support the actions taken by that stakeholder based on their learnings, measuring the business outcomes.

While having a conversation with Chris, I found that every interaction sparks another great story from his vast experience. During a panel discussion at the CX conference, he recalled a simple story about running shorts. He said that buried in the data, they found many athletes asking questions about the size and location of pockets on the running shorts. "Many" in relation to the total number of online shoppers. To measure the scale of an issue, the team had developed a simple multiplier methodology. In other words, if 50 runners were asking a given question, then 1,500 runners likely had the same questions and just weren't asking. Based on this insight, Chris and the CX team worked with the web team to update product descriptions and include an additional photo that shows the pockets. They also worked with retail teams to incorporate this learning in training and coaching for in-store employees. These improvements led to a 30% increase in conversion for the running shorts product category.

Furthermore, after Topbox came into the picture, their analysis of in-app interactions between customers revealed that the instructions for product returns were being misinterpreted, and more importantly, why customers were getting it wrong. The instructions were rewritten to address the specific points of confusion, resulting in a six-point increase in the percentage of returns that were successfully converted to exchanges.

Improvements were made across the business based on the insights produced from the VOC program. Regular reports were sent out to business units enabling them to make customer experience improvements to product, digital, retail, marketing, brand, pricing, public relations, contact center, logistics, and even human resources. No business function was too small, as there was always a customer talking about their experience with that department.

### Hunter Douglas

I also had the opportunity to meet Melinda Keith. Melinda is the senior director of Customer Support at Hunter Douglas, a company that manufactures custom window blinds, shades, shutters, and drapery. In conjunction with their dealer partners, they custom measure, manufacture and install for each order, and offer control solutions that integrate with the modern smart home. Melinda's staff receives more than 125,000 interactions per month, comprised of phone, email and chat. In addition to offering post-call VOC surveys, they are recording, transcribing and analyzing the interactions themselves, using Topbox's AI algorithms. For example, from a transcribed interaction, they can collect brilliant insights in addition to customer sentiment, and can parse this data individually by employee. Melinda is using this data to train and reward employees.

During a roundtable discussion, Melinda shared a story about product discovery uncovered by the data. The daily report showed that installers across multiple current jobs had requested a few sets of shades to be remanufactured. She was able to see that these were coming from the same product line and fabric code, all with a similar issue: fraying. Having this information allowed them to help the product development team to take action. They tested the fabric and realized it was indeed a problem. They informed customers and paused the manufacturing process with the specific fabric while a solution was researched. They put the fabric itself on hold for future orders until the situation could be corrected.

Hunter Douglas has trained their customer support team on how to deal with interactions like these that hint at an emerging issue. Imagine if they didn't have the data? They would likely not fully understand the problem for months. They would continually be sending installers to homes and paying for warranty work.

## CX Tribe

Omni-channel conversation analysis helped runners find the right pair of shorts, and discovered product insights that saved millions.

While this book focuses mainly on using CX data to drive behavior and power business outcomes, you can't ignore the data. An engaged employee will help create two to three times the survey responses and customer insights. This will give you way more data to analyze. Also, don't ignore data that is available from the other channels.

Next, it is time for a couple of epic stories. A top-tier U.S. rental car company is driving behavior at the counter and powering improvement everywhere with an immersive CX 2.0 strategy. Let's find out how that got started and evolved into the epic story it is today.

# CHAPTER SIXTEEN

# A Top-Tier U.S. Rental Car Company

In Chapter 8, we discussed the two types of employees we see most often: the autonomous route-to-market employee (loan officer, real estate agent, doctor, lawyer, insurance agent, etc.) and the hourly employee. In this example, we focus on the counter agent at a top-tier U.S. rental car company, which fits into the hourly employee group.

To comprehend the situation with this company when we starting working with them, you really need to understand the rental car industry. It is not an easy business for smaller comapnies to have success. Issues seem to pile up until they make you scratch your head and ask, "Why would anyone do this?"

First, you have the basic economic issues:

1. The big rental companies buy more vehicles, so their fleet costs are lower than they are at smaller competitors.

2. Massive inventory, multiple locations, high revenues and more capitalized balance sheets afford the larger companies far more favorable financing terms on vehicles as well, often by a factor of two-to-three times less.

3. The business is largely driven by price, making it a tough environment for the smaller companies. If I can rent a Hyundai Elantra from Enterprise for $23 a day, then the small companies are forced to offer their Elantra for the same price or less due to lesser brand recognition.

4. Big companies receive premium airport locations that appeal to busy travelers. Due to high volume, they have more staff and vehicles available.

It is impossible to fix some of the core issues. They are what they are. So, they assessed the state of the business and decided they could benefit from implementing a experience management platform. If you can't compete on operational costs, airport locations, or price, then you have to win by connecting with your customers. In August 2017 our company was asked to join the Request for Proposal (RFP) process.

During the RFP discussions, we learned that they had been using a more traditional NPS model for years. They sent surveys to their customers after the vehicle was returned. Their 2.5% response rate was fairly average for car rental companies. They would receive a monthly report and stare at the negative NPS scores and focus on process improvement where possible. They would also call their location management directly and have conversations about how to increase the numbers. Adding insult to injury, nearly every person on the team was pointing fingers at corporate—the people in the company most removed from the customers—to fix issues that are best resolved on site in real time. In this situation, NPS reports mostly echo what you already know about the business and are already focused on resolving. Therefore, they will have little to no positive impact on the business.

When our company entered the conversation, they asked if we could simply get their happy customers to write reviews online in an effort to mute all of the bad reviews. Up until then, they had no strategy to manage third-party reviews and directories. Unfortunately, their unhappy customers were doing it for them and making them look terrible on most sites.

Our initial proposal focused on a "counter agent campaign,"

since they speak to every customer at pick up. They are the employees who have the biggest impact on customer experience. First, we went to several of their locations and watched the process. We also interviewed counter agents and location managers. Using the information found in discovery, we designed a CX 2.0 strategy.

While the proposal process is confidential, the chief marketing officer at the rental company was concerned about frontline employee measurement. "You're not putting our counter agents in your system," she laughed. "That would take a lot of work and they can turn over pretty fast." But after hearing the entire plan, she agreed to give us a small pilot.

Using our CX 2.0 methodology, this was the plan:

1.   Hire a full-time head of experience that reports to the team. This person works at our corporate office, but travels to the rental companies locations to engage, deploy, motivate, and train.

2.   Add all agents, along with all leaders, into the campaign—the entire hierarchy from counter agent, to location and city managers, to regional vice presidents, to corporate leadership on up to the CEO.

3.   Connect to the their point of sale via API to

integrate transactional data and send each customer a satisfaction survey within minutes after the vehicle is checked out.

4. Create an agent scorecard to include customer satisfaction score, volume of reviews, completion rate and percentage of quality contact information collected from the customer, such as a correct telephone number and email address.

5. Adjust the agents' commissions to drive engagement and behavior, making their customer satisfaction scorecards a key component.

6. At "open contract" (when customers are collecting their car), send a personalized survey from the company and the agent. Ask survey questions relating to items completely within the agent's control, holding them accountable. Friendliness? Helpfulness? Efficiency?

7. Develop happy customer workflows that automatically share the Voice of the Customer (VOC) on the location and company websites and social media pages.

8. Develop unhappy customer workflows that automatically apologize, collect feedback and escalate issues to the correct location, area and

corporate managers with a quick response trigger.

9. Ask all customers to write additional third-party reviews on sites like Google My Business.

10. Deploy a similar campaign at "close of contract" to collect NPS data and additional valuable business intelligence.

11. Develop unhappy and happy customer workflows for the NPS survey, similar to items 7, 8, and 9 above.

12. Use Google, Yelp, Facebook and Infogroup APIs to manage all locations' Name, Address and Phone number (NAP) data across over 100 Tier 1 and Tier 2 websites (Citations).

When we started, they shared some benchmark data from years of using a standard NPS model. It was not good.

**-25**     Net Promoter Score
**2.5%**    Completion rate
**1.8**     Average Google rating across all locations
**25K**     Average number of reviews collected per year
**47%**     Good customer contact data (when they get rental agreements from third-party travel sites, they don't provide accurate contact info.

Third-party sites want the customer's loyalty to remain with them, not the rental car company. When there are long lines and impatient customers, it is difficult to get counter agents to update these fields at checkout).

**70%** The number of their customers that were coming from a third-party travel sites (OTAs) like Priceline and Travelocity. These are their most expensive bookings as it pays commissions to the OTAs of up to 30% of the "Time & Mileage" revenue for each reservation. So, even a small improvement in direct bookings in their "home channels" (i.e., website, mobile app, call center) would improve the bottom line.

The startling numbers listed above were costing them millions of dollars annually.

| **-25** 😟 | ⊘ **2.5%** | **1.8** ★★★★★ Google |
|:---:|:---:|:---:|
| NPS® SCORE | COMPLETION RATE | AVG. GOOGLE STAR RATING FOR +/- 70 LOCATIONS |

| **25K+** | **47%** | **70%** | **2.5%** |
|:---:|:---:|:---:|:---:|
| REVIEWS PER YEAR | GOOD CUSTOMER CONTACT DATA | % OF CUSTOMERS COMING FROM TRAVEL SITES | ALL IN COMPLETION RATE |

Now, let's test our plan against the CX 2.0 Rules.

## The CX 2.0 9 Rules

1. **Focus on the Most Impactful Interactions** - The most impactful interactions are the moment the customer walks up to the counter agent and the moment the customer returns the car. Focusing on these gives us a human-to-human springboard for driving behavior and powering business outcomes.

2. **Start with Behavior** - The campaign provides individual front-line employee measurement, compensation improvements, internal competitions and instant accountability. We mapped compensation, ego, accountability and competitive workflows and dashboards for the counter agent and the managers.

3. **Know and Drive Business Outcomes** - Unhappy customers were controlling the company's online reputation and costing millions in business. Using automation would engage counter agents, make customers happier, collect lots of reviews, enroll customers in loyalty and marketing programs, repair the company's online reputation, and retain employees longer. We also wanted to give them a management layer to celebrate top performers and to create training opportunities.

4. **Wherever Possible, Automate** - Our plan was to automate as much of the strategy as possible, as demonstrated in Rule #3. By connecting to their transactional API and automating all requests, we would set up alerts, complaint resolution, social sharing, ranking, monitoring, and marketing workflows.

5. **Escalate and Resolve Issues** - Automatically alert location, area and corporate management as well as the customer care team instantly when unhappy customer feedback is received. Management would have the authority to resolve any issue.

6. **Manage Content and Consistent Data** - Organize all of their location data (listings management) on key sites such as Google, Bing, Yahoo, and Yelp.

7. **Collect and Share Feedback** - Connect to their location and company social media APIs to share reviews on social and company websites, as well as ask customers to write additional third-party reviews. The program would start with a focus on Google My Business reviews workflows. We would also aggregate online reviews from other sites and share them on their company and location web pages.

8. **Create a Virtuous Cycle** - Focusing on the behavior of the counter agents was our starting point. The plan was to ask customers questions about topics the agent directly impacts, so the agent controlled the results. The campaign's intention was to improve customer experiences, collect more reviews, share them online, get customers to fix the Google reviews problem, clean up customer data, enroll customers in loyalty programs, get more repeat business and direct bookings, and make employees happier so they would be less likely to leave. Retaining employees longer would also reduce hiring and training costs and enhance the customer experience (since a seasoned employee knows the company and the customers better.)

9. **Make Data-Driven Decisions** - This is an ever evolving exercise. The more data we collect, the more we learn, react, and evolve the program. In our last meeting we were focused on happy customer data, loyalty, and marketing as well as unhappy customer trends and systemwide improvements that are needed.

Today, more than two years later, the outcomes and stories could fill their own book. First, I'm happy to report that the chief marketing officer is now a fantastic part of the CX 2.0 tribe. We quickly went from test to full deployment. Without the company's full participation, the results would have never been as dramatic.

When you walk up to the company's San Antonio location counter and talk to Courtney, you are in for a great customer experience. No matter how long you waited in line to talk to an agent, he is going to take great care of you. When you walk away from the counter, it is likely that Courtney will tell you about a survey that you will receive, maybe even before you get in the car. The survey will feature his smiling face and name. Courtney is engaged in the process and is making sure you have a wonderful experience, in part, because the company has integrated his CX 2.0 scorecard into his monthly bonus compensation.

In spite of all the core issues facing a rental car business, Courtney has a 13.6% survey completion rate on the counter agent campaign, confirming the customer's email and address nearly every time for a 94% deliverability rate. He has over 600 personal reviews and a 79 Net Promoter Score. Courtney can control the outcome by providing exceptional service, and he is doing just that. Courtney and the other awesome agents in the San Antonio location have collected almost 4,900 reviews at 4.4 average stars (out of 5.0) in the last 24 months. Before CX, the company had 1.8 stars on Google and a 2% response rate on the old NPS survey. Now, they have 3.8 stars on Google and are improving daily.

This top-tier U.S. rental car company has used CX 2.0 in partnership with their great team and they have become a customer satisfaction company.

> *"Our NPS scores are correspondingly climbing, along with our agents' individual service scores—which is EXACTLY the Virtuous Cycle we seek to create!"*
> — RAC, CEO

Agents are engaged, managers are engaged and the results keep getting better. In one location, for instance, the manager needed to think of a way to really motivate his counter agents to be more involved in the CX program. He wanted to show them that getting surveys representing their great service is just as important and financially beneficial for them as up-selling fuel, insurance, or vehicle upgrades. Agents weren't realizing that commissions they could earn for maintaining their minimum customer satisfaction scores were just as meaningful as selling a toll pass. Hitting the customer satisfaction numbers is no easy task, but he really wanted to show every agent that they could all exceed the minimum expectations.

The manager asked his six agents for a list of things they love to spend money on. One of the counter agents answered with, "Shoes...Air Jordans to be exact." Armed with this information, the manager started calculating how much each individual would make if they had hit their customer satisfaction target, 4.5 stars and a minimum of 10% completion rate. Each month he would send them the dollar amount along with a picture of their loved item showing them they could have easily made that purchase by hitting their number.

Every agent, every month was getting this information. This branch has now been the No. 1 location for customer satisfaction five months straight. At least five of the six agents reach their incentive target every month.

This top-tier U.S. rental car company is now paying meaningful bonuses to every agent that hits their monthly customer satisfaction minimums. Just last month, one agent in Denver earned $2,000 in bonus compensation because of the way she treats her customers.

## CX 2.0 Virtuous Cycle for a Top-Tier U.S. Rental Car Company

A good deployment, like this one, creates a Virtuous Cycle that keeps the business continually improving over time. Here is that cycle:

1. **Drive Counter Agent Behavior** – Personalized surveys and agent scores, along with competition, accountability, ego and compensation, to drive behavior.

2. **Enhance Customer Experience** – Customers are now rating agents 4.5 out of 5 stars on average.

3. **Improve Online Reputation** – Average Google rating went from 1.8 to 3.8 stars in the first two years, across all locations.

4. **Leverage Better Customer Data** – Increased the number of good customer emails from 47% to 91%.

5. **Increase Customer Loyalty** – 70% of their business used to come from travel sites, now it's down to 50%.

6. **Retain Great Employees** – Focusing on great CX leads to happier customers and happier employees.

Here are the results so far:

|  | BEFORE | AFTER |
|---|---|---|

### BEFORE

**-25** ☹

NPS® SCORE

**2.5%**

COMPLETION RATE

**1.8** ★★★★★ Google

AVG. GOOGLE STAR RATING
FOR +/- 70 LOCATIONS

**25K+**

REVIEWS PER YEAR

**47%**

GOOD CUSTOMER CONTACT DATA

**70%**

% OF CUSTOMERS
COMING FROM TRAVEL SITES

**2.5%**

ALL IN COMPLETION RATE

### AFTER

**+24** ☺

NPS® SCORE

**10.8%**

COMPLETION RATE

**3.8** ★★★★★ Google

AVG. GOOGLE STAR RATING
FOR +/- 70 LOCATIONS

**250K**

REVIEWS PER YEAR

**91%**

GOOD CUSTOMER CONTACT DATA

**49%**

% OF CUSTOMERS
COMING FROM TRAVEL SITES

**18.4%**

ALL IN COMPLETION RATE

While each of these stats show ridiculous improvement, especially since it all happened so quickly, let's focus on the last statistic. An all in completion rate of over 18% in the rental car business is way outside of any reasonable limit— it's nearly impossible. This is not funny math, and it is not a trick. We are not measuring only rewards members. We are not measuring only those who opened or clicked on the survey. They are incentivizing survey responses. We send a request to every customer and we get 18.4% of them to complete a review. When counter agents are engaged in making customers happy, customers will do them a favor and complete the survey.

We have two customer-facing campaigns, the first is open contract and the second is closed contract. As of the time that this book is being written, we average about 10% and slightly higher on closed contracts. If you remove the customers that complete both (duplicates are roughly 3% of the total), we get over 18% of unique customers to complete at least one survey.

All of this improvement happened in only the first two years after going all in and deploying a CX 2.0 strategy that was customized to their business. And their numbers will continue to improve.

Now, we come full circle. In the past, businesses collected the VOC to gain insights, create reporting, update processes and track progress. Today, we know that this alone is not enough. Data begins to age moments after it's collected. The data must immediately be put into motion to drive outcomes.

Imagine how valuable it is for a location manager to call, text, or email a customer who gave an unfavorable rating on their survey while they are still in possession of the rental car. "We heard your feedback. We can fix your issue. We apologize for the inconvenience." Who does that? How impactful can that be to the final score?

They embraced CX 2.0 and turned their employees into brand ambassadors and customers into their #1 marketing asset online. They have better data, more loyal customers and happier employees. And, they have nearly 10x the reviews to put into reporting and give to management. The biggest difference is that today they can virtually guarantee improvement month-over-month in these numbers.

> *"Our CX program is driving real behavior change that we are seeing in the bottom line."*
> — RAC, CEO

## CX Tribe

With hourly employees, compensation is the primary behavioral driver, provided the employee's performance can impact the results. In the example we looked at in this chapter, the bonus compensation is meaningful and so are the results. There's 8X the response rates and nearly 10X the number of reviews annually. A 50-point increase in NPS scores, hundreds of thousands of new organic clicks and a 20% lift in organic buisiness.

The outcomes of a properly deployed CX 2.0 program will have a dramatic impact on your business. To maximize results, the transaction data must be automated via a connection to your point of sale (POS) system. The surveys must be personalized to the individual front-line employee. Surveys need to go out in real time—the faster the better. Complaint resolution needs to be thorough and automated (mostly). Sharing of reviews needs to be automated via APIs and widgets. The more automation, the more success.

If instead of hourly employees, they were route-to-market employees like a loan officer, how would the behavioral deck of cards (Ego, Compensation, Competition and Accountability) be shuffled?

CHAPTER SEVENTEEN
# New American Funding

*"Anything a mortgage company can do to help the loan officers build trust in the communities they serve is vitally important."*

— RICK ARVIELO, CEO OF NEW AMERICAN FUNDING

At New American Funding (NAF), a mortgage lender headquartered in California with more than 180 locations across the country, their primary route-to-market employee is the loan originator. Loan originators build relationships with real estate agents, CPAs and attorneys. They focus on winning their local markets to originate new business.

A proper CX 2.0 strategy for autonomous, route-to-market staff (loan originators, real estate agents, insurance agents, etc.) looks somewhat different than a program built to manage hourly employee behavior. In this case, you have professionals that engage in much longer transaction cycles where the one-to-one relationship is very meaningful.

When our company started the conversation with New American Funding, they already had several in-house developers focused on this problem. In fact, they had a working system for collecting reviews. While this can be a barrier, it can also be a benefit. Firms like NAF that are already focused on customer feedback and reputation are more receptive to the CX 2.0 conversation. They have seen the power of reviews and have their own statistics to compare. We were lucky to convince Rick and Patty Arvielo, the founders of New American Funding, to run a pilot so we could show them the impact of a good CX 2.0 program as it compared to their homegrown system.

In this situation, the problem was pretty simple: NAF wanted a way to manage their online reputation and turn their happy customers into their #1 marketing asset and create a lot of new local business for their originators. For this implementation, we focused primarily on collecting and sharing reviews.

Using our CX 2.0 methodology, this was the plan:

1.  **Key Point of Contact** – Identify a key point of
    contact within NAF and a dedicated resource to
    manage and move workflows, as well as add,
    remove and train users.

2.  **Company Hierarchy** – Add all agents, locations,
    regions and corporate offices, along with all
    marketing and CX leaders, into the campaigns and
    alerts.

3.  **Automate Data Connections** – Connect to their
    loan origination system. At funding of the loan,
    automatically request feedback from the customer
    on behalf of the loan officer.

4.  **Survey Build** – When the loan closes, send a
    personalized survey to the borrower aliased from
    their loan originator. Ask survey questions specific
    to the items completely in the loan officer's control.
    Any additional questions (non-loan originator
    specific) should be excluded from the loan
    originator's rankings.

5.  **Partner Surveys** – At funding, also automatically
    request feedback from real estate agent partners
    to enhance existing relationships and create new
    ones.

6. **Share Reviews** – Connect to company websites, social media pages and relevant third-party reviews sites (focusing on Facebook, Twitter, LinkedIn, Zillow and LendingTree for all Loan Officers, Branches, Regions and Corporate locations.) Build workflows that will allow sharing to all possible loan originator profile pages and location and company pages.

7. **Third-Party Reviews** – Ask all customers to write additional third-party reviews using a flexible workflow on sites like Google My Business, BBB and Credit Karma.

8. **Reply to Reviews** – Pull all reviews from all locations, such as Google and Facebook, into a single dashboard so the NAF team can easily monitor and respond.

9. **Dashboards** – Develop an agent, branch, region and company dashboard for real-time stats, leaderboards and sharing. Create quick edits, bulk edits and quick add features for the NAF management team.

10. **Drive Competition** – Create a loan officer scorecard and real-time leaderboard to include customer satisfaction rating, volume of reviews and completion rate. Rank agents using modified

Bayesian inference[1] and include ranking offset for completion percentage.

11. **Resolution Workflows** – Develop unhappy customer workflows that automatically apologize, collect feedback and escalate issues to location, region and corporate managers. Also, notify NAF's customer care team and map the transaction ID so they can easily pull file notes prior to calling the customer.

12. **Location Data** – Use Google, Yelp, Facebook and Infogroup APIs to manage all locations' NAP data (citations) across 100+ Tier 1 and Tier 2 websites.

Just by reading the list above, you can see it meets and follows the CX 2.0 rules closely. This exercise is important when building your strategy. Always match your outcomes and execution plan to the nine rules.

1. **Focus on the Most Impactful Interactions** – Most of NAF's business comes from local referrals and via relationships with real estate agents. The post-closing survey that supports this effort through sharing workflows is the obvious choice.

---

[1] http://bit.ly/CX20_Bayesian

2.  **Start with Behavior** – The campaign provides for social sharing automation for loan officer profiles. This creates new business (compensation) and an ego response. The strategy also includes a real-time loan officer ranking (competition) that is visible when users login. It has real-time complaint resolution and escalates all issues (accountability).

3.  **Know and Drive Business Outcomes** – New American Funding and their loan officers were already doing an exceptional job building relationships and serving their customers. The primary objective was to collect and share more reviews and publish content online so that NAF loan officers and locations can build their reputation and win searches in their local markets.

4.  **Wherever Possible, Automate** – By connecting to their transactional API and automating all requests, we created a strategy which includes automated alerts, complaint resolution, social sharing, ranking, monitoring, and marketing workflows.

5.  **Escalate and Resolve Issues** – Our platform instantly alerts location, area and corporate management, as well as the NAF customer care team when unhappy customer feedback is received.

6. **Manage Content and Consistent Data** – The entire location hierarchy is added to our platform and we publish accurate listings data to more than 100 listings websites. We also provide a single dashboard that aggregates reviews and allows the company to reply to any review for any location.

7. **Collect and Share Feedback** – Reviews and sharing workflows are most important in this strategy. We automate the review collection process and request feedback from the borrower, co-borrower, buyer's agent and seller's agent. This turns a single transaction into four possible reviews. Additionally we pull in reviews from Zillow, Google, Facebook and other third-party websites and add those to our sharing and management workflows. We automatically share the reviews on loan officer, location and company social media pages (Facebook, LinkedIn, and Twitter) as well as the loan officer company websites on the NAF domain. Reviews enhance listings on sites like LendingTree and Google, as well as profile pages on marketing software and CRMs. We have more than 20 of these connections and share the average NAF review 10-12 times.

8. **Create a Virtuous Cycle** - The program drives behavior because it allows loan officers to create new business using the true voice of their happy

customer with complete automation. The loan officers are continuously asking for the ranking algorithm because they want to win. The system collects customer feedback at an extremely high rate and shares that feedback in as many places as possible, powering the company's reputation online. It connects to Facebook Business Manager and allows NAF to build custom audiences and run client loyalty campaigns.

9. **Make Data-Driven Decisions** – NAF's response rates from customers and agents is over 50%. For purchases, they often include a borrower, a co-borrower, a buyer's agent and a seller's agent. This means they have more than two responses on the majority of their purchase transactions.

Before New American Funding deployed a CX 2.0 strategy, their 1,000+ loan officers had fewer than 4,000 reviews across websites like Zillow, Google and BBB. They were missing out on many opportunities to broadcast the voice of their customers, with fewer than 500 Google reviews for nearly 180 locations.

After two years of using a proper CX 2.0 strategy, the results are the best in the business—by the time you read this, the numbers will have grown substantially. As of January 2020, NAF has nearly 95,000 reviews, including over 7,167 on Zillow, plus another 3,504 on Google My Business and

Credit Karma. Their average score across all these reviews is 4.88 stars and a Net Promoter Score of 89. Their survey completion rate is over 54%.

| | | |
|---|---|---|
| **94,391 Reviews** | **4.87 Rating** | **Our Company** |
| **3,217 Reviews** | **4.8 Rating** | **Google My Business** |
| **24,144 Reviews** | **4.9 Rating** | **LendingTree** |
| **7,167 Reviews** | **4.9 Rating** | **Zillow** |
| **287 Reviews** | **4.9 Rating** | **Credit Karma** |

NAF took charge of their online reputation. They were already creating WOW-worthy customer experiences, they just needed to activate their customers with a proper CX program.

Professionals using the CX 2.0 methods are reporting a 13% average increase in new business from the automated workflows. Additionally, our data shows that roughly 66% of the business that comes into NAF, as well as other lenders and real estate companies, is referred. However, more than 30% of these referred customers are searching for the professional online prior to calling. They are using social proof and reviews to validate the referral. In this environment, you must support your route-to-market employees by helping them create an amazing online presence and win in their local markets.

## CX Tribe

Is the campaign you a planning to develop focused on the autonomous route-to-market employee, like at New American Funding, or hourly employees? It is possible that you have an opportunity within your company to run both types of campaigns. At NAF, they use reviews to win in their local markets and grow revenues. They also have a Voice of Employee (VOE) annual campaign. Do you have a distributed retail environment similar to New American Funding? If so, this epic story should be a good roadmap for a successful design.

Next, let's name the campaigns and create some basic CX 2.0 outlines for each. It takes surprisingly little effort for companies to have multiple automated campaigns running simultaneously.

CHAPTER EIGHTEEN

# Designing Your CX 2.0 Strategy

The top-tier rental car company simply wanted simply wanted to encourage happier customers to write Google Reviews. Now, they are transforming their business with a CX 2.0 deployment. New American Funding wanted to promote their loan originators. Today they have a marketing machine that is helping them win locally in every location.

Recently, I received a survey request from Apple about an employee. It was a short form survey that clearly was designed to drive employee engagement and behavior. At the end of the survey it asked me if I had time to answer more questions. In other words, they did the behavioral survey first, and then offered me the opportunity to complete the long form. BRILLIANT!

Kudos to Apple and their experience management platform. While I have no insight into how the survey impacts employee compensation, or if it is driving competition, accountability, or ego—it appears to be executed effectively. One thing that could improve is its timeliness. I received this request for survey a few days after my purchase. I assume this means that they are using some kind of batch process. If the survey hit my phone while I was walking out of the store, the response rates would improve significantly.

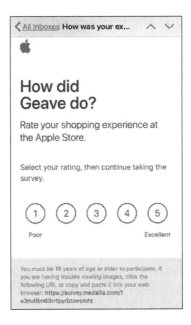

Like in the Apple example, a company with high transaction volume should begin seeing results in hours and a measurable impact on business outcomes in just a few weeks. For large enterprise builds, software partners will likely dedicate a full-time resource to design, develop and deploy your strategy. Post-launch, the full-time resource would lead engagement, user additions and removals, payroll integration and reporting, training, replies and other requirements of the plan.

Below is a design guide using the Apple example. I am not certain if they have all of this automation, but it could easily fit. Hopefully the guide below can help you design your strategy, especially for human interactions.

### Design Checklist

| | |
|---|---|
| **Campaign Title** | Apple (I made this up from the example above, using CX 2.0 ideas). |
| **Interaction Measured** | Retail Purchase Check Out. |
| **Player** | Sales Person. |
| **Secondary Player** | N/A. |

### CX Outcomes

☐  **#1**  **Improve Service Levels** - Create a scorecard to measure quality data, completion rate and star rating. Integrate results into weekly and monthly competitions. Add CX to bonus compensation.

☐ **#2** **Automate Complaint Resolution** - When a customer is unhappy, escalate the issue to local management immediately.

☐ **#3** **Collect Long Form Survey/Insights** - If the customer is willing, offer them the long form survey and collect product and service insights.

☐ **#4** **Improve Contact Info** - Add data scrub to the checkout workflow and measure it as an employee scorecard component.

☐ **#5** **Boost Marketing Efficiency** - Add all happy customers to a custom audience using pixel automation.

☐ **#6** **Win Locally** - Thank all customers for their feedback and ask them to take a second to leave their comments on Google. Direct them to the local location's GMB.

☐ **#7** **Automate Business Listings Management** - Since all locations are a part of the strategy, automate the publishing of listings data.

☐ **#8** **Reply to Reviews** - Give location managers the ability to reply to happy customers, as well as escalate the reply requirement for unhappy customers to the customer care team.

☐ **#9** **Integrate Management** - Include NPS or overall satisfaction into the manager's scorecard. Incentivize location managers with location competitions and bonuses based on continual improvement and minimum standards.

☐ **#10** **Improve Culture and Retention** - Use VOC to celebrate employees. Share the best stories socially. Highlight employees in company forums. Make the best review a part of daily meetings.

## Survey Questions

☐ **Question #1** How did [employee name] do? Rate your shopping experience at the Apple Store.

☐ **Question #2** Please share your feedback with [employee name].

☐ **Question #3**    Do you have time for more questions?

☐ **Question #4**    Switch to long form survey.

## Survey Workflows

☐ **Connection Type**    Automated via API.

☐ **Primary Request Method**    Immediate email on checkout, trigger email simultaneously when receipt is emailed. They will be expecting the email receipt, so they will likely open both emails.

☐ **Secondary Request Method**    SMS — Wait 24 hours and send a text with a business purpose and a survey link.

☐ **Tertiary Request Method**    N/A.

☐ **Personalization**    Personalize request from Apple about employee.

☐ **Humanized** — Use employee name (maybe photo) in survey.

☐ **Share Rule** — Ask customers to share socially over 4 stars.

☐ **Auto Share 1** — Automatically share all reviews on Apple web pages.

☐ **Automate Audience** — Build custom audiences using Facebook Pixel automation. Create five audiences based on rating.

☐ **Post Survey Request** — Ask all customers (happy and unhappy) to write Google Reviews for their local store.

☐ **Other Request** — Automate additional business process such as adding to rewards program, confirming contact information like address and phone number, registering a product on the website.

For additional details on how to set up escalations, dashboards and logins, and other manual components, please see the Appendix on page 217.

I would be surprised if Apple has gone as far as described above, or even if it all fits into their strategy. Hopefully much of the detail tracks alongside your own plans. After you have designed the checklist for your campaign, I recommend simplifying it to a small list of execution items and using your preferred project management software to carry out the strategy.

A complete strategy will take no more than 90 days to design, develop, board and launch. Also, be wary of software companies that are large billing machines. If a company wants to charge you big money for consulting to design and develop your strategy, call others. Recently I heard a story of a company that paid over $1M to customize a CX collection program, averaging less than 1,000 responses annually.

With hundreds of companies claiming to solve pieces of the puzzle, how do you choose the right partner(s) for you? When it comes to technology, companies are often split between "build it" or "buy it". With hard-earned dollars on the line, the main questions are often: How do I avoid the pitfalls? What are the best ways to adopt new technologies for my company? How do I execute? Whether you're taking notes, attending conferences or asking for success stories, every movement is essential in order to get the maximum value from each vendor relationship. Remember each situation is unique and the only way you'll know that you're making the right choice is by doing your research because only you know your company best.

### CX Tribe

It may be difficult to get HR, sales, marketing, and operations teams all aligned in a single, interconnected strategy. The truth is, if you're asking that question, it's likely not going to happen as fast as you'd like. However, if you have the ultimate goal in mind, it's OK to "box check," provided you choose partners that have solutions to solve the current problem and will help you achieve your future goals.

In software we call this "land and expand." You may have to run your own "land and expand" strategy in-house. For instance, the head of HR may not want you to disrupt their Voice of Employee (VOE) program. But after they see the success you are having on other initiatives, you can de-risk their decision process and get them onboard with an integrated solution.

When building your CX 2.0 strategy, it will have multiple campaigns and outcomes—start with one. A good CX 2.0 strategy should take no more than 90 days to design and deploy. Assign a full-time resource from your team to focus on it.

Next, let's do a quick recap of some of the more common examples discussed and create one from scratch for a well-known pharmacy brand.

CHAPTER NINETEEN

# Your Hometown Pharmacy

Great companies are running immersive CX strategies all around us—many that we interact with every day. It is fascinating that we don't adopt the same ideas to improve our businesses. If you are buying a book, renting a room, or hailing a car, you may be a participant in some company's behavioral masterpiece.

## Companies who put their "get better" first...

Throughout the book we have explored several examples of companies who put their "get better" first and are winning:

**Airbnb** drives behavior of 2.5 million hosts who manage more than 6 million properties and creates great customer experiences for more than 2 million people nightly with their 5-star CX host program.

**Uber** manages the behavior of over 3 million contract drivers and creates great experiences for 75 million riders with their 5-star CX driver and rider programs.

**A Top-Tier U.S. Rental Car Company** manages the behavior of hundreds of counter agents and creates better customer experiences which improve their online reputation with their 5-star CX counter agent program.

**New American Funding** drives great customer experiences, online reputation and a lot of new local business with their 5-star CX loan officer program.

**Amazon** manages more than 5 million sellers, improving the quality of products and service levels for 26 million transactions a day with their 5-star CX program.

Each of these companies are CX pioneers in their respective markets. It's no mistake that their CX strategies are creating new business, improving customer loyalty and positively impacting products. The list highlights five very different companies, all using a CX program to drive behaviors and power great business outcomes. Arguably, the same opportunities exist in every industry.

### CVS - Your Trusted Hometown Pharmacy

Here is an example with CVS Pharmacy and how they might drive employee and customer behavior to power great business outcomes and become a local leader in every location.

(I will disclose that we have spoken to CVS and their CX leadership is focused on an extremely comprehensive strategy to be rolled out soon. I will update this from time-to-time as their initiatives progress.)

Here is the scenario: you are the CX leader at CVS Pharmacy. You are trying to combat the growth of online Rx orders that are eating into your volume and impacting profits. In addition to the revenue you might have earned on filling the prescription, you lose an opportunity for that customer to purchase other items when they come in to pick up their order.

You have 10,000 local locations and want the local pharmacist to build relationships with customers and truly become the hometown pharmacy you are meant to be. How would you create a CX 2.0 strategy to achieve this objective and get people off of the internet and back into your stores?

First, we did a little research to create a starting point for the deployment and a discussion of where the strategy can have the biggest impact on the business:

### The Good

- 10,000 local pharmacy locations and 1,100 walk-in clinics
- 300,000 employees
- 5 million customers served daily
- 62 million Rewards Program members

### The Bad

- Average Google My Business listing has six reviews and 3.1 stars
- Complaints about wait times and impersonal pharmacists are driving current reputation
- Inconsistent citation data on Google, company sites and listings
- Bad online location naming includes CVS, CVS Pharmacy, (location) CVS, CVS 24 Hour Pharmacy and CVS Health
- Top eight Google search results for "CVS reviews" are not good

Can a CX 2.0 strategy drive the trusted hometown pharmacy reputation you are looking for? Absolutely! This one is easier to design than you may think. Even the items listed under "The Bad" can be fixed relatively quickly. The power for CVS starts with those 300,000 employees, but focuses on the counter in the back of the store. Within 12 months of CVS deploying an immersive CX 2.0 strategy, they should be the #1 reviewed pharmacy in the U.S. and have their employees and customers fully engaged in the "trusted hometown pharmacy" conversation.

Here is how they might roll it out:

### No human interference

CVS currently asks for customer feedback via a 17-digit code on their receipt— definitely not user-friendly. If they were to update to an automated digital method with no inconvenient steps, it would yield higher survey responses and higher customer satisfaction.

CVS should connect to the point of sale and digitally ask every customer for feedback, but not ask the same customer more than once every 90 or 120 days.

### Measure and engage employees

Put a photo of the smiling pharmacist who helped them in the feedback request. Measure each pharmacist with scorecards, rankings and an instant feedback loop with great customer stories continually flowing in for motivation. Here is actual feedback from a customer using their current survey process:

*"This survey is not user-friendly. I am not gonna waste time to figure out how to leave feedback. Anna you were great, I was trying to leave you a good review but I cannot figure out the survey."*

### Escalate any negative feedback

Apologize and automatically resolve negative feedback and contact unhappy customers with escalation workflows, involving customer care and upper management. In every instance, seek to turn the detractor into a promoter. What is the lifetime value of a customer with just their pharmacy purchases, not to mention non-pharmacy items they add to their basket on their way out the door.

### Share feedback

Use marketing and social post automation to share happy customer feedback. Ask every customer to write reviews on key third-party review sites, like Google. Aggregate all online reviews and share them on company and location web pages.

### Properly manage all locations' information on key sites

Use listings management best practices to standardize all titles across more than 100 listings sites for all CVS locations. Clean up NAP data (name, address, phone, as well as website, hours, photos and category) on all listings.

What are the outcomes CVS will enjoy? How fast will they see results?

First, CVS will see more engaged employees. Days into the program, when the pharmacists start to read their customer feedback, they will become more involved in connecting with their customers and their stories.

Next, they will begin to identify with the good stories and see themselves as a CX leader, as opposed to just the sporadic reactions to upset customers.

Within the first six months, CVS will see completion percentages at four-to-five times the national average and thousands of new 5-star reviews on Google. CVS will have business intelligence on locations and front-line employees with consistent listings data on all websites. They should see hundreds of thousands of new organic click actions from relevant keyword search traffic.

> *"Almost instantly, employees and customers will get involved in the Trusted Hometown Pharmacy conversation. This is an immersive and deliberate strategy intended to drive specific outcomes with automation: that is the power of CX 2.0".*

The CVS story would be epic. While I can't be certain, I assume that the folks at CVS are already focused on many of these outcomes. But do they understand that a complete CX 2.0 program drives exponentially better outcomes by creating a Virtuous Cycle that starts with the human interactions at the counter?

CVS is a local pharmacy, and customers do have great experiences. They just need a strategy to connect, engage and drive the "hometown pharmacy" conversation in store and out of store.

## CX Tribe

This week, it is likely that you will help a company (like Uber, Amazon, or Airbnb) drive behavior and power their brand. It is also likely that your voice will impact someone's buying decision, even someone you have never met. It is probable that someone you have never met has impacted your buying decisions recently. How many employees and customers can you activate to do the same for your business? Are you designing a campaign for your company? Take a moment to test your strategy against the CX 2.0 Rules:

1. Focus on the Most Impactful Interactions
2. Start with Behavior
3. Know and Drive Business Outcomes
4. Wherever Possible, Automate
5. Escalate and Resolve Issues
6. Manage Content and Consistent Data
7. Collect and Share Feedback
8. Create a Virtuous Cycle
9. Make Data-Driven Decisions

Finally, the new experience category will integrate and automate many business systems. The next Salesforce will come from the experience category.

CHAPTER TWENTY

# The Next Salesforce

As of January 2020, Salesforce had a market cap of over $162 billion. They are one of a kind. They didn't invent CRM, they invented cloud CRM—perfecting the enterprise platform with endless integrations. Some companies now build their entire offering on Salesforce. They have more employees (35,000+) than the population of many towns.

It's a pretty brazen statement to say that the next Salesforce will come from the experience category, but it is definitely possible. The addressable market in the current "reputation" space is in the tens of billions in potential revenue, and it is just beginning to take shape. Hundreds of software and consulting companies are checking boxes for customers one at a time. This has given us some good visibility into the "what comes next?" conversation.

That's where we will finish this book: What's next?

First, the category is not reputation—the category is experience. The new experience category will integrate and automate many business systems, upholding the three pillars: data, behavior, and outcomes.

1. **Data** — Collecting, aggregating, parsing, and analyzing experience data of all kinds, these companies often use artificial intelligence to analyze data and help others make business decisions. This is where most high-cost consultants and premium products live.

2.  **Behavior** — Driving engagement and behavior of employees. SAP calls it HXM (Human Experience Management) and focuses on developing a more engaged workforce to power business outcomes. This is also a high-cost group of providers and products.

3.  **Outcomes** — Third-party reviews, business listings, citations, sites, social sharing and monitoring are just a few of the products you'll find in this pillar. There are hundreds of companies fighting for attention here, and the offerings are extremely commoditized.

Most companies are focused on one or two of these pillars. Some companies host complete platforms for human-to-human interactions. However, no company has developed a platform that comprehensively solves all of these.

### The Experience Platform

Remember the idea that started our conversation in Chapter One?

> *"Experience management is not a list of individual problems and solutions. It is a single puzzle. When put together properly, each piece works far more efficiently than it possibly could as an individual solution."*

All three pillars, products, and experience outcomes will eventually live in a single platform. Now that you know the story, it should be easy to visualize the future of the experience category. Just like Salesforce, it will be an enterprise platform with countless integrations.

Being part of the future experience platform will be critical in order to scale, as enterprises become more sophisticated and begin to connect the puzzle, demanding a single integrated platform.

Here is a description of many of the products that will be available in the enterprise experience platform:

> **Journey Mapping** – A tool that allows a company to map, prioritize and activate workflows, products, people and drive outcomes within journeys.

### Customer Journey Map

> **Customer Experience** – Collecting and analyzing customer experience data from customers, chat, Q&A, social engagement, telephone calls, messaging and websites.

**Employee Experience** – Collecting, threading and analyzing employee experience data on recruiting, boarding, training, annual reviews and offboarding journeys. Sharing employee feedback socially and on relevant third-party sites.

**Employee Engagement** – Building programs and gamifying employee behavior and engagement to improve the customer experience.

**Listings Management** – Managing consistent NAP data on hundreds of third-party websites like GMB, Yahoo, Yelp, Bing, and YP. Activate simple methods for replying to customer-facing reviews for multiple locations.

**Third-Party Reviews** – Directing customer and employee review traffic to relevant third-party review sites like Google. Reply to all reviews, across all locations.

**Complaint Resolution** – Automating complaint resolutions workflows including customer care escalations, alerts, responses, archives, reporting, and replying to unhappy reviews.

**Optimized Websites** – Creating site templates that are search engine optimized with consistent NAP data, rich content about products and services offered, as well as aggregated customer reviews.

**VOC Marketing** – Sharing voice of the customer on blogs, social media, industry-specific third-party review websites and news websites to share company stories at scale.

**Audience Building** – Marketing automation for building social audiences, social marketing and SEM. Pixel and retargeting to maximize a custom audience for both Google and Facebook.

**Mentions Monitoring** – Monitoring the internet for company mentions and intelligence to understand consumer trends.

**AI and Analytics** – Leveraging experience insights with reporting, AI and analytics dashboards to find and resolve CX issues, benchmark performance and make data-driven decisions.

There are many more pieces of the puzzle than those listed above. It will be a sales, marketing, operations, HR, and compliance platform that drives business improvement with automation. Happy employees, motivated to "Create WOW" for fellow team members and customers; proud to deliver exceptional experiences powered by tremendous automation. Loyal customers sharing their "WOW" experiences everywhere—growing their reach, SEO, and top-line revenues. A highly automated platform that will impact and improve culture, brand and ultimately, share price.

## CX Tribe

Thank you for spending your valuable time to explore our CX formula. It is my sincere hope that this book has created WOW for you and will have a big impact on your future customer and employee experience strategies. Design your strategy, partner with the right vendors, and Create WOW.

## APPENDIX

Design Guide: Additional Examples

### <u>Escalations — Unhappy Customers</u>

☐ **After Unhappy Response**    Apology page.

☐ **GMB No Gating Policy**    Offer GMB workflow.

☐ **Escalation Rule**    All detractors.

☐ **Escalation Team**    Alert employee, location manager, and customer care.

☐ **Customer Alert**    Escalation email to customer.

☐ **Post Review Rule**    Offer all unhappy customers the ability to continue the conversation.

## **Dashboards & Reporting**

☐ **Login**　　　　Integrate employee results into current intranet or employee portal. Give location, district, regional and corporate managers CX dashboard login with permissions based on their location reports/teams.

☐ **Ranking**　　　Employee ranking by city and district.

☐ **Reply**　　　　Reply to reviews dashboard based on permissions set.

☐ **Users**　　　　Add/edit users, integrate with active directory.

☐ **Listings**　　　Listings by location.

☐ **NPS**　　　　　NPS Report tracking progress by location, district, region, company.

☐ **Other**　　　　Survey stats reports.

☐ **Employee**    Employee scorecard and
payroll reporting/integration.

☐ **Complaint**    Complaint resolution report and
workflows dashboard.

## Manual Components of the Strategy

☐ **Reviews**    Reply to every review.

☐ **Unhappy Customers**    Contact every unhappy
customer within 0-2 hours.

☐ **Payroll**    Use reporting for pay
and bonuses.

☐ **Reward**    Add monthly and annual
customer satisfaction
awards.

☐ **Training**    Promote Top
Performers to train
others.

## Other Possible Additions

☐ **Online Monitoring**     Mentions monitoring
                            software.

☐ **Single Sign On**        Use APIs for Apple
                            intranet integration.

☐ **Google Retargeting**    Add Google retargeting to
                            reviews pages.

☐ **Customer Care API**     Map file notes and
                            review to Apple Care
                            customer service team.

☐ **Marketing**             Add marketing, retention,
                            and referral workflows.

## AUTHOR BIOGRAPHY

 Scott Harris is a CEO, keynote speaker, and author of *"Create WOW Customer Experiences: CX 2.0."*

If you ask Scott what he does, he will likely describe himself as a "Dad" and as his company's "Chief Storyteller." Whether at home with his children and grandchild, or at work with a growing family of 70+ employees, he tries to bring passion, joy, and direction into the lives of everyone around him.

Scott has 20+ years of experience building enterprise technologies. In 2015 he launched SocialSurvey, a fully automated experience platform that helps businesses put feedback data in motion to drive behavior and power real-time outcomes. Scott is focused on people and relationships, with a goal to Create WOW moments for customers, employees and partners.

Connect with Scott on LinkedIn at www.linkedin.com/in/sharris15/.

## ACKNOWLEDGMENTS

Nobody has been more important to me in the pursuit of this project than my family. Thank you for the early mornings, and for the long weekends of writing at the office. Rebecca, Bailey, Mason, and Charlie, you are the air I breathe. Also to the rest of our family of nine, thank you so much for your love, patience and support Emma, Ruby, Matt and Everett.

This work would not have been possible without all of the research, design, editing and content support provided by my fantastic team:

**Emma Monro**
**Erin Fox**
**Stevie Burger**
**Craig Pollack**
**John Jackson**
**Amy Li**
**Jessica Smiley**
**Rebecca Harris**

I am grateful to all of those I have had the pleasure to work with on this project. I am especially indebted to the following individuals who contributed their personal experiences:

**Erin Clark of Horace Mann**
**Brittany Hodak**
**Christopher Stark and Jonathan Moore of Topbox**
**Melinda Keith of Hunter Douglas**

And thanks for our following clients:

**Jonathan Gwin of American Financial Network**
**Michael Fusco of Fusco & Orsini Insurance Services**
**Scott Davido**
**Rick and Patty Arvielo of New American Funding**

I was inspired by brand mastermind Marty Neumeier, corporate culture entrepreneur Tony Hsieh, and business strategist Fred Reichheld to write this book.

For those of you who have attended our company's marketing and culture Summit over the years and are members of our Partner Advisory Board: your input has been instrumental in roadmapping the future of our company, my personal knowledge, and this WOW work.

And to the real WOW creators, my team. Additional recognition goes to those who have given their time to contribute to all the value found herein:

**Dennis Ackley**
**John Bachmann**
**Laurie Courtwright**
**Jason Frazier**
**Paul Gambs**
**Sarah Harris**
**Peter Herlan**
**Chris Herr**
**David Kawata**
**Patrick McCauley**
**Philip Seelenbacher**
**Charlie Vezzali**
**Jeff Weddell**

# INDEX

**Accountability**    70, 84, 87, 115, 122, 167,173, 177, 183, 189

**Airbnb**    91-95, 200, 207

**Amazon**    26, 27, 36, 37, 41, 149, 200, 207

    Effect    36, 37

    Prime    41

**American Financial Network**    119, 120, 226

**Apologizing**    104, 116

**Audience Building**    96, 105, 213

**Automation**    53, 55, 66, 76, 78, 83, 87, 97, 103, 107, 109, 111, 127, 143, 145, 167, 177, 183, 185, 191, 192, 195, 204, 205, 213

**Backlink(s)**    55, 106, 137

**Better Business Bureau**    105, 181, 185

**Behavorial Driver(s)**    83, 84, 178

**Boarding**    72, 97, 152, 212

**Bounce Rates**    82, 86, 90

**Brand**    10, 11, 15, 18, 19, 21, 22, 24, 25, 28, 32, 49, 52, 69, 80, 84, 105, 106, 135, 143, 149, 152, 155, 157, 161, 176, 198, 207, 214, 226

**Call center(s)** 81, 129, 151, 166

**Campaign** 32, 53, 69, 70, 73, 84, 85, 88, 103, 138, 144, 163-165, 167, 169, 170, 175, 180, 183, 185, 187, 191, 196, 198, 207

**Checklist** 191, 196

**Citation Signals** 126, 133, 140

**Collect Feedback** 89, 115, 164, 182

**Company Hierarchy** 89, 180

**Compensation** 56, 84-86, 108, 151, 167, 170, 172, 173, 177, 183, 189, 191

**Complaint Resolution**
*see also* Escalate 97, 104, 107, 115, 168, 177, 183, 192, 212, 219

**Content** 29, 62, 96, 124, 131-133, 136, 168, 183, 184, 207, 212

**Contractors** 70, 79, 80, 88

**Conversion** 96, 108, 156

**Counter Agent**
*see also Employee, Hourly* 46, 73, 160, 163, 166, 167, 169, 170-173, 175, 200

**Create WOW**
*see also WOW* 9, 30, 213, 215, 226

**Create WOW Summit** 30, 226

**CRM** 88, 184, 208

**Culture**                          10, 15, 18, 21-25, 27-30, 32,
                                     51, 69, 70, 80, 152, 193, 214,
                                     226

**Customer**

    Care, Success           55, 117, 121, 122, 151, 168,
                                     182, 183, 193, 204, 212, 217,
                                     220

    Data                    84, 88, 97, 149, 169, 173

    Experience

    *see also CX*           9-11, 37, 42, 45, 47, 48, 52-
                                     54, 56, 67, 68, 71, 73, 78-80,
                                     82, 84-88, 90, 91, 94-97,
                                     100, 109, 111, 112, 122, 127,
                                     140, 143, 144, 145, 147, 148,
                                     150, 151, 153-157, 159, 163,
                                     166, 169, 170, 171, 173, 175,
                                     176, 177, 179, 180, 182,
                                     185-188, 191, 196, 198, 199,
                                     200-203, 205-207, 213, 215,
                                     218, 225

    Happy                   12, 13, 15, 19, 28, 29, 31, 35,
                                     36, 37, 39, 47, 48, 81, 105,
                                     106, 118, 130, 144, 145, 147,
                                     150, 151, 162, 164, 165, 169,
                                     175, 179, 184, 192, 193, 195,
                                     204, 213

Loyalty                  27, 48, 49, 51, 52, 80, 81, 88,
                         96, 117, 150-152, 167, 169,
                         173, 185, 200

Satisfaction             25, 32, 45, 49, 51, 52, 56,
                         81-84, 88, 102, 107, 108, 111,
                         164, 171, 172, 181, 193, 203,
                         219

Unhappy                  28, 31, 37, 39, 54, 55, 81,
                         101, 104, 107, 109, 111, 115,
                         117, 118, 121, 123, 145, 162,
                         164, 165, 167, 168, 169, 182,
                         183, 192, 193, 195, 204, 212,
                         217, 219

Voice of the             155, 164, 213

**CVS Pharmacy**         201, 202

2.0 Rules

**Dashboard(s)**         85, 86, 105, 167, 181, 184,
                         196, 213, 218, 219

**Data**

at Rest                  53, 54, 56

in Motion                53, 54, 56, 74, 95, 223

**Detractors**           50, 51, 115, 217

**Distance**             125

**Ego**                  84, 85, 167, 173, 177, 183,
                         189

**Employee**

|  | Engagement | 14, 15, 76, 98, 188, 212 |
|---|---|---|
|  | Frontline | 103, 163 |
|  | Hourly | 84, 160, 177, 179, 187 |
|  | *see also Counter Agent* | |
|  | Route-to-market | 84, 160, 177-179, 186, 187 |
| **Enterprise** | | 9, 12, 17, 155, 161, 191, 208, 211, 223 |

**Escalate**

| *see also Complaint Resolution* | 55, 61, 87, 97, 110, 114, 117, 120-123, 168, 182, 183, 192, 193, 204, 207 |
|---|---|
| **Experience Economy** | 32, 34, 37, 39 |
| **Facebook** | 51, 104, 121, 135, 144, 145, 165, 181, 182, 184, 185, 195, 213 |
| **Fusco & Orsini** | 140-143, 226 |
| **Gamification** | 84 |
| **Gating** | 144, 209, 217 |
| **Google** | 12, 13, 144, 169, 185, 188, 195 |

|  | Algorithm | 125-127, 134, 139 |
|---|---|---|
|  | Local Pack | 141 |
|  | Local Search | 79, 126, 127, 140, 144 |

My Business (GMB)          18, 79, 83, 126, 127, 131,
                           135, 136, 140, 144, 165,
                           168, 181, 185, 186, 202

Reviews                    12, 13, 16, 144, 169, 185,
                           188, 195

**Horace Mann**            68-73, 226

**HR**                     17, 95, 96, 98, 109, 198

**Human Interference**     102, 203

**Hunter Douglas**         155, 157, 158, 226

**Insurance**              39, 68, 73, 111, 140-143, 160,
                           171, 179, 226

**Keyword**                132, 140, 141, 143, 205

**LendingTree**            134, 145, 181, 184, 186

**Likeliness to Refer**

*see also NPS*             44-46

**Listings Management**    77, 78, 135, 168, 192, 204,
                           212

**Loan Officer/Originator**

*see also Mortgage*        41, 145, 160, 177, 178,
                           180-185, 187, 200

**Local Business**         38, 124, 129, 133, 135, 142,
                           143, 179, 200

**Location Data**          18, 77, 78, 124, 136, 168,
                           182, 185, 209

**Loyalty Programs**       81, 169

| | |
|---|---|
| **Marketing** | 30, 55, 76, 81, 95, 96, 108, 151, 157, 163, 167-169, 176, 179, 180, 183, 184, 192, 204, 213, 220 |
| **Monitoring** | 18, 97, 106, 118, 121, 136, 168, 181, 183, 210, 213, 220 |
| **Mortgage** | |
| *see also Loan Officer/Originator* | 111, 120, 131, 134, 145, 178, 179 |
| **Motivation** | 84, 87, 107, 163, 171, 203, 213 |
| **Multi-Location Brand** | 143 |
| **NAP Data** | 133, 136, 165, 182, 204, 212 |
| **Net Promoter Score (NPS)** | 14, 42-53, 84, 85, 149, 162, 165, 170, 171, 177, 193, 218 |
| **Newport Coffee Company** | 39 |
| **On-Page Signals** | 126, 131, 140 |
| **Online Reputation** | 38, 39, 80, 149, 150, 167, 173, 179, 186, 200 |
| **Overall Satisfaction Question** | 45, 193 |
| **Partner Surveys** | 180 |
| **Passives** | 45, 49-51 |
| **Pay-per-click** | 139, 140, 142 |
| **Pharmacy** | 199, 201-206 |
| **Point of Contact** | 180 |

**Prominence**                      125

**Promise**                         20, 27-32, 69, 81

    External             30, 31

    Internal             28-32

**Promoter(s)**                     31, 44, 49-51, 55, 87, 109,
115, 119, 121, 123, 204

**Recruiting**                      18, 29, 32, 70, 72, 88, 96, 98,
151, 212

**Referral(s)**                     25, 33, 41, 48, 49, 52, 96,
104, 105, 124, 143, 146, 147,
182, 186, 220

**Relevance**                       125

**Reply to Reviews**                107, 118, 140, 145, 181, 184,
193, 212, 218, 219

**Reputation Management**           13, 75, 76

**Restaurant(s)**                   38, 126, 152

**Retarget**                        105, 151, 213, 220

**Retention**                       18, 29, 32, 49, 55, 88, 96,
151, 152, 193, 220

**Rewards**                         52, 149, 150, 151, 175, 195,
202

**Reviews**                         15, 17, 28, 33, 36, 38, 72,
76-79, 81, 83, 92, 94, 96, 102,
104, 106-109, 112, 121, 126,
130, 131, 135, 139, 140-147,
151, 152, 155, 162, 163, 165,

|  |  |  |
|---|---|---|
|  |  | 166, 168, 171, 176, 178, 180, 182, 184, 187-190, 197, 204, 206, 207, 212, 214, 215, 220-222 |
| **Sales** |  | 95, 96, 109, 191, 198, 213 |
| **Salesforce** |  | 75, 207, 208, 211 |
| **Scorecards** |  | 15, 66, 82, 83, 86, 90, 105, 108, 138, 164, 170, 181, 191, 192, 193, 203, 219 |
| **Scoring Model** |  | 10, 48, 83, 90, 147, 151, 152 |
| **Search Engine** |  | 84, 125, 129, 132, 133, 135, 212 |
|  | Results Page | 132 |
| **Sentiment** |  | 14, 77, 126, 143, 158 |
|  | Analysis Data | 33 |
| **SEO** |  | 55, 94, 96, 132, 214 |
| **Social** |  |  |
|  | Media | 55, 89, 104, 117, 122, 140, 145, 146, 155, 164, 168, 181, 184, 213 |
|  | Proof | 37, 38, 81, 94, 96, 186 |
|  | Sharing | 89, 104, 168, 183, 210 |
|  | Selling | 97 |

**Software**                13, 15, 17, 75, 152, 184, 191,
                             196, 198, 209, 220

**Starbucks**               52
**Subway**                  22
**Third-Party Websites**    15, 18, 41, 55, 104, 117, 118,
                             121, 140, 144-146, 166, 181,
                             184, 204, 210, 212, 213
**Topbox**                  155, 157, 158
**Top Performers**          82, 87, 94, 107, 167, 219
**Train(ing)**              27, 28, 55, 72, 96, 97, 118,
                             156, 158, 163, 167, 169, 180,
                             191, 212, 219

**Transaction**             103, 109, 111, 139, 168, 179,
                             182-184, 185, 190, 200
        Cycles              180
        Data Integrations   103, 164, 177
        Management System   101, 103

**Uber**                    111-15, 200, 207
**Verifying Business Location**  128
**Virtuous Cycle**          56, 64, 88, 95, 147, 148, 150,
                             151, 153, 169, 171, 173, 184,
                             206, 207
**Win Local**               188, 192

**Words of Affirmation**         85, 86

**Workflows**                    123, 144, 145, 148, 149, 150,
                                 151, 164, 165, 167, 168, 180,
                                 181, 183, 184, 192, 211, 217,
                                 220

    Automated                104, 107, 119, 120, 121, 186

    Manual                   105, 111, 121

    Secondary                83, 104

    Survey                   115, 194

    Resolution, Escalation   119, 182, 204, 212, 219

**Yahoo**                        14, 105, 135, 168, 212

**Yelp**                         14, 28, 41, 128, 129, 133,
                                 134, 135, 152, 165, 168, 182,
                                 212

**Zappos**                       21, 26, 27, 28, 51

**Zillow**                       145, 181, 184-186

Made in the USA
Columbia, SC
30 June 2020

12388378R00130